The Taming Of The C.A.N.D.Y.* Monster

*Continuously Advertised Nutritionally Deficient Yummies!

a cookbook by Vicki Lansky

illustrated by Lynn Johnston

Book Trade Distribution:
Publisher's Group West
Emeryville, California

the book peddlers

deephaven, mn

Other titles by Vicki Lansky:
Feed Me! I'm Yours
Kids Cooking
Fat-Proofing Your Children

Practical Parenting Tips for the First 5 Years
Practical Parenting Tips for the School Age Years
Toilet Training
Welcoming Your Second Baby
Traveling With Your Baby
Getting Your Baby to Sleep and Back to Sleep
Birthday Parties
Dear BabySitter Handbook

The Best of Vicki Lansky's Practical Parenting Newsletter

101 Ways to Tell Your Child "I Love You"

KoKo Bear's New Potty
The New Baby at KoKo Bear's House
KoKo Bear and the New Sitter
KoKo Bear's Big Earache (Preparing for Ear Tube Surgery)

Sing-Along as you Ride-Along (Book and Tape)
Sing-Along Birthday Fun (Book and Tape)

Illustrations by Lynn Johnston
Cover and text design by MacLean & Tuminelly

First Printing February 1978
Tenth Printing March 1982
Revised, Eleventh Printing March 1988
Copyright ©1978, 1988 by Vicki Lansky

20   19   18   17   16   15   14

Published by
The Book Peddlers, 18326 Minnetonka Blvd., Deephaven, MN 55391
(612) 475-3527
ISBN-0-916773-07-8 (quality Paperback)
ISBN 0-916773-08-6 (Library edition)

Printed in the United States of America

TO
DOUG AND DANA
My tireless tasters who always insure
my life is kept in perspective.

Acknowledgements

**A cookbook develops in the kitchen
as well as out of the kitchen.**

My special thanks go to:

Claire Prosser...for recipe development and testing
Dr. Jack Anderson...a knowledgeable nutritionally-oriented, pediatric
  dentist
Dr. Mitch Einzig...a personable pediatric gastrointestinal specialist
Vernal Packard...a sharing food scientist from the University of
  Minnesota
Bev Kees...an erudite editor
Janet Sadlack...a microwave maven
Margaret Burgess...for her ABC's on our IBM
Bob Burgess...for his significant book title contribution
Ellen Gold...a friend and home economist who married a milk-
  intolerant doctor
Julie Surma...for editorial expertise
Recipe thanks go to: Kathy Johnson, Meredith Berg, Friske Louw, Jill
and Julie Segal, Kathleen Dalton, Jan Bakken, R. Henne, Elizabeth
Holey, Aunt Betty (Booth)

Contents

Continuously **A**dvertised **N**utritionally **D**eficient **Y**ummies

Contemporary Glossary
Of Kitchen Terms

Feeding kids is no small chore. Sometimes you feel you've been transported to another world with a language all its own. If the following list of kitchen definitions sounds familiar, then we are all speaking the same language and we are not really on strange soil after all!

Appetizing	anything advertised on TV
Apple	tooth fairy's delight
Bananas	tropical disease which affects a parent as a child swings into 6th month of a food jag
Boil	a point parents reach when hearing the automatic "yuk" before food is even tasted
Brown	status of a towel after hands are washed
Casserole	a combination of favorite foods that go uneaten because they are mixed together
Chair	spot left vacant by mid-meal bathroom visit
Chop	a Karate move
Concession	a C.A.N.D.Y. stand where a parent usually concedes

Cookie (last one)	an item that must be eaten in front of a sibling
Crust	the part of a sandwich saved for the starving children of (check one): China, India, Africa or Europe
Dessert	the reason for eating a meal
Drain(ed)	what is felt in the presence of a tense child
Evaporate	magic trick performed by children when it comes time to clear the table or wash the dishes
Fat	microscopic substance detected visually by children on pieces of meat they do not wish to eat
Fiber	nutrient found out-of-doors such as in a sandbox
Fish	a form of protein with "too many bones"
Floor	place for all food not found on lap or seat
Fork	eating utensil made obsolete by the discovery of fingers
Fried Foods	gourmet cooking to kids
Frozen	condition of children's jaws when spinach is served
Fruit	a natural sweet not to be confused with dessert
Funnel	a bath tub toy
Germs	the only thing kids will share freely
Grate	a verb describing the feeling caused by a whinney voice
Hungry	constant condition of both well-nourished and mal-nourished children

Ingredient	item called for in a recipe of which one is inevitably missing
Jelly Bean	the only "vegetable" all kids will eat
Juice	a football star who also runs through airports
Ketchup	a condiment that other foods are eaten with
Kitchen	the only room not used when eating a crumbly snack
Kitchen Shears	the only scissors left because the kids haven't found it suitable for craft projects
Knead	the action children take to separate us from our dough
Liver	a food that affects genes creating a hereditary dislike
Lollipop	a snack provided by people who don't have to pay your dental bills
Maple	a tree that has given its name to an artificially flavored syrup
Melt	what happens inside us the first time our child makes us breakfast
Metric	a system of measurement that will be accepted only after 40 years of wandering in the desert
Measuring Cup	a kitchen utensil which is stored in the sandbox
Milk	a widely used floor cleaner
Natural Food	food eaten with unwashed hands
Nutrition	a secret war waged by parents using direct commands, camouflage and constant guard duty

Napkin	any worn cloth object, such as a shirt or pants
Macaroni	material for a collage
Peanut Butter	staff of life
Pinch	an action done to cheeks which children find unsavory
Plate	breakable Frisbee
Pot Luck	when children set the table
Refrigerator	a very expensive and inefficient room air conditioner
Saliva	a medium for blowing bubbles
Soda Pop	Shake'n Spray
Sucker	a parent who lets kids eat dessert who haven't finished their main meal
Snack	the meal lasting all day
Table	a place for storing gum
Table Leg	a percussion instrument
Thirsty	how your child feels after you've said your final "good night"
Unstick	when a fast melting popsicle departs from its stick
Vegetable	a basic food known to satisy kids' hunger...but only by sight!
Water	popular beverage in underdeveloped countries
Yukky	half the vocabulary of a child
Yummy	other half of vocabulary of same child

Nutrition is a Matter of Parenting

C.A.N.D.Y. (Continuously Advertised Nutritionally Deficient Yummies), sweet desserts and fast food restaurants have a magical appeal to my children. With hundreds of millions of advertising dollars aimed directly at them, I am not surprised. I know what my kids would do with the grocery money if they did the shopping, and where they would like to eat if I didn't plan on cooking—and it's not at Grandma's!

It's very difficult for parents concerned about the quality and safety of the foods we buy to know whether we are making nutritious food selections. Most of us don't really believe that all these overly sweetened, salted and fatty/fried foods we're warned against are really all that bad. After all, who ever heard of someone dying from an overdose of chocolate chip cookies? And even the "experts" don't agree. How is it possible to deal intelligently with the flood of conflicting information on nutrition? The apparent choices are either to make a leap-of-faith into the health food camp or to continue with suicidal bravado down the aisle filling our grocery carts with the usual selection of junk foods.

I find myself in the middle of this dilemma. My young son was the original C.A.N.D.Y. monster and his younger sister a close second. I have come to believe that many packaged convenience foods are not my best nutritional buy. Yet, as a busy, non- kitchen-oriented mother of two, I don't think I should have to trade good taste and convenience for better nutrition. How does one decide which foods to buy and which to avoid?

The more I read, the more I recognize how publicity will give credibility to any "new" information that comes along before time or testing gives us a clearer picture of the real story. Oftentimes information is theory, not fact. Testimonial evidence (*I took this—it cured that*) is not accepted by the medical and academic community. How and where does one find the *Truth*—if it is even known?

Doctors provide us with few specifics unless we're on a special diet. Their advice is generally limited to the admonition, "Eat a balanced diet!" But what does that really mean? They say it is a diet emphasizing protein foods, dairy foods, fresh fruits and vegetables, and whole grain foods, and that no one food contains all the nutrients we need, which is why variety is essential. True! But they usually fail to add that good health is not encouraged by unnecessary consumption of candy, cakes, cookies, chips, highly sweetened cereals, pop, powdered and canned soft drinks, etc.; and that kids (and parents) should lighten up on fried foods, pasta, white bread and rolls. They check children's tonsils but not their junk food consumption. When was the last time your pediatrician asked about your child's diet?

Nutrition is seldom studied in-depth in most medical schools. One doctor told me that his major nutritional education in medical school covered scurvy and rickets—two diseases he has yet to see among his patients. Doctors are trained to treat illness, not to prevent it.

According to Jane Brody of the *New York Times*, a child needs more nutrients per pound of body weight than does an adult. If a child is given too many high-calorie foods that are low in all nutrients but sugar— soft drinks, cookies, cake, candy and the like—he or she may quickly fulfill caloric needs without consuming enough of the essentials.

This puts the responsibility right back on us as parents. We are, after all, the shoppers and providers; one of the most important ways we nourish our children is by the food we serve them. Nutrition relates directly to growth, health, learning ability and general well-being.

For years parents, as well as consumer advocates and nutritionists, have been bothered by the substances ADDED to the foods we eat. The word "additive" conjures up a negative image. Actually, an additive is *anything* added in manufacturing, preparing, treating or storing food. The same vitamin A you eat in a carrot becomes an additive when it is extracted and put in another product. Sugar dropped in your iced tea or coffee is an additive. The flavorings of sugarless gum are additives as are the colorings that go into cheese. Additives receiving the most attention are those that make possible all the convenience foods we've come to depend upon. Additives are needed for flavor, texture, appearance and shelf-life. They facilitate food preparation, make many foods readily available and maintain food values by preventing spoilage. On the other hand, some are used to disguise inferior processing, conceal inferior ingredients and deceive us by making fabricated foods appear to be the real thing.

BUT, ARE ADDITIVES DANGEROUS? I'm not the expert, but it appears that most additives are safe; a few are questionable. One way to establish nutritional priorities lies in an examination of the quantity of additives we eat. Food scientists agree that anything in great quantity can be dangerous, sometimes cancer-causing, even lethal. Salt can be toxic and so can caffeine when consumed in excessive dosages. Many of the foods we ingest have a natural toxicity but are dangerous only in excess. While no additives we eat have been proven to cause cancer in humans, some studies using animals indicate possible danger.

Since I have taken quantity as a key criterion of safety, let us examine the quantity of additives we actually ingest:

Additive	1975 per capita annual consumption*
white refined sugar	90 pounds
corn syrup and dextrose	24 pounds
	114 pounds total sugars
salt	15 pounds
saccharin	7 pounds
everything else	10 pounds

Source: "Food consumption, Prices and Expenditures—'75 supplement;" U.S. department of Agriculture. "Processed Foods and the Consumer;" V. Parkard, University of Minnesota Press, 1976.

By the way, the average per capita consumption of refined sugar in 1900 was between 20-60 lbs. Official government records were not kept in 1900 for this item so estimates vary. Until recently, and with the exception of NutraSweet, the greatest controversies surrounded those additives far down on the consumption list. The most commonly consumed additives actually are the various sugars and salt.

The "everything else" referred to in the additive chart included yeast, pepper, mustard, sodium bicarbonate, citric acid, MSG, and an additional 27 or so additives which account for 9 of the 10 pounds listed. That last pound of the 10 accounts for colorings, emulsifiers and preservatives.

Sugar

The sugar we are referring to here is the white, refined variety made from cane or beets. Sugar which occurs naturally in foods will not be included in this figure. These figures indicate that your family of four will consume over 450 pounds of caloric sweeteners, if your diet is typical. How can this be? Think back to the number of bags, boxes and bottles you have carried into your home. Nearly every one of them contains added sugars: sodas, sauces, crackers, cakes, sherbets, ice creams—as well as cereals, bread, dressings and condiments.

There are many ways to say sugar, if you haven't already discovered this fact. There is brown sugar, confectioners' sugar, corn syrup, dextrose, fructose, glucose, maltose, mannitol, molasses, sorbital and honey.

Sugar is 100 percent pure as advertised. Pure calories and nothing else! Sugar offers NO vitamins, minerals or trace elements. This refined carbohydrate is used by your body as energy or stored as fat. We need some of this usage but not in the quantities we have come to use. Sugar, per se, does not contribute to growing strong and healthy bodies.

While there are many claims as to other dangers of sugar in our diet, most professionals today will agree that sugar has two obvious negatives—it leads to tooth decay and weight problems.

While I accept the negatives intellectually, I am not able to completely eliminate refined sugar from my diet or that of my children. I find that there are many parents who share my dilemma. We are at one place intellectually and another in reality. So I deal with this fact by saying that, while none is probably best, LESS is at least BETTER.

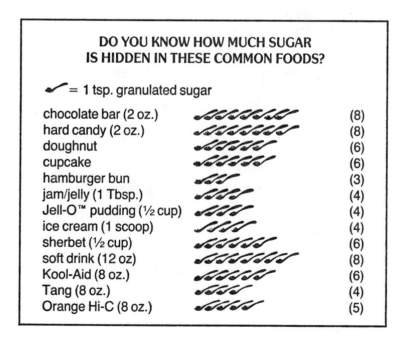

DO YOU KNOW HOW MUCH SUGAR IS HIDDEN IN THESE COMMON FOODS?

= 1 tsp. granulated sugar

chocolate bar (2 oz.)	(8)
hard candy (2 oz.)	(8)
doughnut	(6)
cupcake	(6)
hamburger bun	(3)
jam/jelly (1 Tbsp.)	(4)
Jell-O™ pudding (½ cup)	(4)
ice cream (1 scoop)	(4)
sherbet (½ cup)	(6)
soft drink (12 oz)	(8)
Kool-Aid (8 oz.)	(6)
Tang (8 oz.)	(4)
Orange Hi-C (8 oz.)	(5)

Reducing Your Use of Sugar

Here are some "handles" I have found helpful in reducing my family's sugar intake:

- Decrease the amount of sugar called for in a recipe. In other recipe books, you can decrease a recipe at least by a ¼ cup of the sugar called for without affecting texture.

- Adding extra vanilla flavoring will often compensate for the missing sugar in most any recipe. (See box.)

- Look for recipes that call for less sweetening (all types), not more (such as you'll find in this book and *Feed Me I'm Yours*).

- Don't treat dessert as the final act of every meal. I know one family that serves dessert only twice a week—on weekends!

- Read labels while grocery shopping, or even after you get your purchases home. This may help change your shopping habits.

- Screen children's food requests in the grocery store. A treat can be a piece of fruit or a pack of sugarless gum.

- Don't just say "NO!" Explain the whys. Try to remember to add, "No, because I love you and I want you to grow up to be strong and healthy."

- Discuss TV ads aimed at children. Explain to your children the company's motivation and possible half-truths mentioned.

- Try to decrease your reliance on packaged foods. A bit of extra thought and planning is involved here.

- Use sugar substitutes—in moderation. (See pages 11 and 49.)

- Keep convenient portable snack foods on hand. A fruit plate on the table, nuts in a jar, cut-up vegetables in the refrigerator cooler, and pieces of cheese in a plastic bag in the refrigerator.

- *MOST IMPORTANT!!!* Don't keep C.A.N.D.Y. in the house. That's the only way to insure that junk food is not a major part of your children's daily caloric intake.

More and more parents are not allowing their children to be exposed to refined sugar products. These people feel very strongly that their children don't crave and/or demand C.A.N.D.Y. as the children grow older. Many tell me these foods often seem too sweet and are not missed. But I have seen the other reaction, too.

I myself did not feel as strongly about what my children ate when they were infants as I did as they grew older, so I always worked at changing our food choices and taste preferences. My children never cared for what I broadly refer to as "health foods." They rejected the taste and texture of many of these foods. And I rejected the extra cost. Yet they love whole wheat bread, nuts, fresh fruits and hard cheeses. You *can* buy healthy foods at any local supermarket.

Vanilla—A Surprising Sugar Substitute

Vanilla is actually the fruit of an orchid. The vanilla bean has no taste or odor until it's cured. Pure vanilla extract is made from vanilla beans and diluted alcohol. Imitation vanilla is made with synthetic vanillin and will usually be labled as "vanilla flavor."

Just a drop is needed. Some new ways to use it that you might not have previously considered are:
- Add to sour cream or yogurt.
- Sweeten chocolate, tea or even coffee.
- Mix into unsweetened applesauce.
- Put into the batter of pancakes, French toast or waffles so you will need less syrup toppings.
- Spread a bit over a half-grapefruit.
- Add to cottage cheese with a dash of cinnamon.
- Add a drop to milk used in cold or hot breakfast cereals to reduce or eliminate the need for added sweeteners.
- Use extra drops in baked goods if you like a sweeter flavor.

NutraSweet, the brand name for aspartame, has become a popular sugar substitute. See page 49 regarding its use in drinks. Direct questions you may have for its use to the NutraSweet Center, in Skokie, IL. at 1-800-321-7254.

Honey

Honey has been touted by health food enthusiasts as the healthy answer to the sweet tooth. Interestingly, honey has more calories and is sweeter than refined sugar. Many honey enthusiasts are convinced it is a superior food nutritionally. The nutritional value may be sizeable for bees, but the amount available for human use is small. While not advisable for use if your child is under 1 (it may be a cause of toxic infant botulism), you may wish to use honey as your sugar choice because:

- It metabolizes more slowly—rather than with refined sugar's lightning speed—it is easier on one's insulin and blood sugar level.

- Its cost and (for many) its taste are self-limiting.

- As a spread on bread, it has less fat than butter.

- Because it is sweeter than sugar—less is needed.

Brown Sugar

Brown sugar is a mite better than white refined sugar but only a "baby step" so. The brown comes from a trace of molasses added. Originally brown sugar was sugar with the molasses not completely processed out, but today it is made by returning some of the molasses to regular refined sugar. Still, the molasses does give it a bit of extra food value. Brown sugar even has slightly fewer calories than white sugar.

Your best course of action regarding sweeteners is moderation. We all tend to think we live moderately. The best way I can suggest to test your sugar consumption is to serve your family—for just one day—*NOTHING MADE WITH REFINED SUGAR*. I think you will find it very frustrating. You will have to read every label because you can take nothing for granted in our pre-sweetened world.

Salt

Salt is the second most prevalent additive in our diet. Salt seems to be in everything, as the person on a salt-free diet soon finds out. And the salt added to most packaged foods is usually not the iodized salt that prevents goiter caused by an iodine deficiency of the thyroid gland. Packagers don't add salt for healthy reasons—just taste reasons.

Salt is important in the regulation of our internal fluid balance. Originally used to preserve foods, salt is used now mainly as a flavor enhancer. In fact, it really is a cultural taste habit which has grown to such proportions that it has become an actual threat to our health.

Salt (which is sodium) when taken in excess, which Americans are guilty of, is a primary cause of hypertension in adults. Hypertension, related to heart disease and stroke, affects more than 20 million people in this country. At an annual per capita consumption rate of 15 pounds, we are each consuming at least the equivalent of one round 26 ounce container of salt monthly, or 4000 to 5000 milligrams a day. This is twenty to thirty times the amount we need daily. Nutritionists agree that we should have no more than 200-300 milligrams of sodium a day, which is a bit more than a ¼ tsp.—and that means from all sources both naturally occurring and as additives. Studies have shown that people who use very little salt are practically free from high blood pressure. Now, since you purchase only one to three boxes of table salt a year (and then usually for playdough recipes), you can imagine how much salt must come from packaged and restaurant foods.

In many ways I find it harder to deal successfully with salt than with sugar. Despite the fact that salt is used infrequently in our home and that salt is used infrequently in cooking (it is required in baking because its chemical interaction with yeast controls the rising), I'm still sure that we consume too much of it. We avoid obvious items such as potato chips and French fries but I know we consume excess sodium every time we eat cheese, nuts (most commerical varieties are salted unless otherwise labeled), canned soups, pickles or diet soda. Even most city water supplies contain some sodium. According the the book, *Salt: The Brand Name Guide to Sodium Content* from CSPI (Workman, 1983), 75 percent of our sodium comes from packaged goods. Obviously, the more you avoid packaged convenience foods, the more salt you will avoid. Most recipes that call for salt do so out of tradition. Now is a good time to start changing this cooking habit. Even if salt were never added to foods, we would probably get all we need because sodium occurs naturally in many foods such as milk, meat, eggs, tomatoes and raisins, to name just a few.

Keep in mind that while fresh meats and poultry are relatively low in sodium, this is not the case with processed ham, bacon, sausage and hot dogs. Fresh fish is low in sodium but canned fish, such as tuna, is high.

If you are not ready to do without table salt completely, try LITE SALT which is equal parts potassium and sodium chloride (normal table salt). Or you may wish to experiment with NoSALT, CoSALT or Morton's SALT SUBSTITUTE which are all entirely potassium. Read these labels carefully as excess potassium intake has its drawbacks, too.

Sea salt isn't any healthier for you than regular table salt. The additional minerals that come with sea salt are quite insignificant because most of them are removed when it is purified for human consumption. Going heavy-handed with any salt still adds more to your sodium-laden diet than you need.

Begin to use other seasonings to replace salt. Better-for-you flavor enhancers are lemon juice, vinegar, onion, chives, herbs, and garlic. If you buy powdered garlic, do be sure it is garlic powder, not garlic salt.

Other Additives

Labels tell an astonishing story. Our food seems to be "filled" with additives. Anything other than the base ingredient—and usually that, too—must be listed on the label. These additives may be natural or chemical in origin. Natural additives include salt, sugar, wheat germ, etc. Chemical additives can be a combination of real foods or laboratory duplications. But chemicals are the stuff everything is made of. All the nutrients of our diet—the proteins, carbohydrates, fats and vitamins—are chemical compounds. Ascorbic acid is Vitamin C and vitamin C is ascorbic acid. Natural vanilla flavoring, however, does not have the same chemical base as artificial vanilla flavoring. All additives, natural or fabricated, are regulated by the Food and Drug Administration (FDA) and are restricted as to their use and quantity in various foods. Despite the fact that most additives are safe, it has been a cause of concern for consumers to note that the FDA has changed its mind on occasion and has banned certain additives previously considered safe. For a complete, and easy to read discussion of additives, read *The Complete Eater's Digest and Nutrition Scoreboard* by Michael Jacobson (Doubleday, 1985).

Additives and Hyperactivity in Kids

In the 1970s Dr. Benjamin Feingold, an allergist, first published his findings that artificial colorings and flavorings can cause an "allergic" reaction in children known as hyperactivity. Since most parents feel that their children are hyperactive—at least those of us who prefer a quieter existence—what better motivation does one need to follow his prescribed diet? Dr. Feingold's studies have never been duplicated to the satisfaction of the medical and scientific community though many parents who followed his diet recommendations felt it beneficial—some have felt it is miraculous.

Hyperactivity also includes a syndrome called Attention Deficit Disorder (ADD). A child with ADD (which is ten times more common in boys than girls, by the way) shows several of the following characteristics:

- has difficulty organizing work and gives the impression that he or she has not heard the instructions;
- frequently calls out in class;
- has difficulty waiting his or her turn in group situations;
- makes impulsive errors; or
- is easily distracted.

Sugar in the diet, surprisingly, is a behavioral depressant. Caffeine in soft drinks and chocolate is the stimulant children react to.

Discovering whether diet, counseling or medication will help your child will require some research on your part and consultation with your pediatrician. You may wish to read *The Hyperactive Child, Adolescent and Adult—Attention Deficit Disorder Through the Life-Span* by Dr. Paul Wender (Oxford University Press, 1987) and Dr. Benjamin Feingold's book *Why Your Child is Hyperactive* (Random House, 1975).

For more information on hyperactivity and children write for a free pamphlet entitled "Facts About Childhood Hyperactivity," NICHD, P.O. Box 29111, Washington, D.C. 20040.

For additional information about hyperactivity and diet, you can contact the Feingold Association, PO Box 6550, Alexandria, VA 22306 or phone (703) 768-FAUS.

Fats and Cholesterol

When *Taming Of The C.A.N.D.Y. Monster* was first published in 1978, parents were worried about additives, not fats. In less than a decade, this concern has shifted. Now we read article after article on fats and cholesterol telling us not to predispose our children to heart disease and overweight. You will find a complete discussion of this topic in my book, *Fat-Proofing Your Children* (Bantam Books,1988), but I do want to remind you here that a certain amount of fats are *necessary* for growth and development in young children. Please do not put a child under the age of two on skim milk, for example. Not every child is built the same and *thin-is-in* is the aesthetic of the day but it doesn't mean your child is healthier than the next, if skinny or chunky. Consider carefully before cutting calories from your child's diet. Don't put a growing child on a restrictive diet unless you are working with a doctor or nutritionist. Be moderate in your abstinence from fats just as in everything else.

If your diet is "saturated" with fats, here are some ways of cutting down without cutting out:

- Buy leaner cuts of meat and remove all visible fat.

- Serve meat less often than you do chicken or fish.

- Refrigerate sauces, soups or gravies before serving. As fat cools, it rises to the top and hardens and is then easy to remove.

- Skim fats from dishes as they cook with a bulb baster.

- Use nonstick skillets to cut down on fat used during food preparation.

- Broil, stew, stir-fry, steam or broil foods rather than frying them.

- Buy natural peanut butter that lets the oil float to the top. Pour off the oil before beginning to use jar. Use peanut butter more often than cream cheese as a spread on crackers and veggies.

- Remember that chicken franks contain less fat than beef or pork franks.

- A bagel has less fat than a croissant.

- A baked potato can be softened and mashed with milk rather than butter. It can be topped with cottage cheese or yogurt for a change of pace from sour cream.

- Make your own "French fries" by cutting up potatoes that you bake on greased cookie sheets and that you turn as they brown.

Fats are tricky because they are more calorie-dense than sugar. For instance, a teaspoon of maple syrup will not have as many calories as a teaspoon of butter or margarine. So get in the habit of using less shortening and commerical salad dressings. Don't serve three sausages or slices of bacon where one, on occasion, will do. Be conservative in your use of egg yolks and don't eat high fat and fried meals at fast food restaurants too regularly.

Foods that go uneaten cannot nourish. In selecting recipes for this book, an important criterion has been kid acceptability. Three things make foods taste good: sugar, salt and fats. I have tried to use recipes that are consistently lower in refined sugar, but it has not always been possible. Some recipes contain more sweeteners than I like to serve but these at least have some nutritional advantage over C.A.N.D.Y.— the foods they are meant to replace. Salt is only used in recipes where I have thought it important. I haven't been as successful in reducing fats in recipes. It will be necessary for you to use your judgement in the number and frequency of recipes you choose to make and serve.

My selections are intended to give you a range of alternatives from which to choose, not to earn you a certificate of nutritional purity (whatever that may be). One must weigh cost, preparation time and nutritional value against what will actually be consumed.

For those of you who are struggling to make intelligent market (grocery, that is) decisions, I hope this book will help. Selecting and preparing good foods for one's family is not an easy task. We carry our own food prejudices based on what our mothers fed us, the reality of what our spouses want on the table, what our children will conde-scend to eat and what our pockets can afford.

We are a new generation of parents whose *nutrition* consciousness has been raised. Most of us are not health food afficionados but concerned parents who still wish to experience good tasting food without sacrificing the health of our families.

Brown-Bagging It: School Lunches

A short while ago you were leaving your child with a bottle and a sitter. Now he or she is leaving you with lunch in hand for nursery school, kindergarten or grade school. More often than not, Mom's lunch will be preferred, if not actually demanded. You will probably hit upon a few favorites plus a variety of fruits and vegetables that will make your child's approved list. Do not be surprised when you discover that much trading and switching goes on over lunch tables. It's the *American Way*. But too often we hear that sandwiches end up in the waste-basket, desserts are eaten first, and "side dishes" are left on the side. If you are getting this kind of feedback, the time has come for a re-evaluation of what you are packing for lunch.

Your child's choice of a lunch pack container will be determined by the peer group. Sometimes the fashionable lunch box is in, and other times it's the brown paper bag. There are pros and cons for each. The box, while more expensive, keeps sandwiches from getting squished and holds a thermos. The bag is cheaper but may be considered unecological. On special outings, a bag is a better selection than the forgettable-in-the-excitement lunch box.

Variety may not be important to every school-age child. One child will insist on peanut butter sandwiches for lunch every day while another prefers a variety. As for Mom, there are advantages to each approach and nothing absolute about either.

The lunch you pack should include:

- a Protein Rich Food
- a Fruit or Vegetable
- Something Extra (*I hate to classify it as dessert*)
- a Beverage
- Food For Thought (*optional*)

A Protein Rich Food

Lunch bags are not legally required to contain sandwiches. Besides, the bread, when it is made primarily of white flour, may be more of a filler than a nutritious food. Consider packing in small plastic bags:

Cheese—a hunk, slices or string cheese (mozzarella)

Nuts—a variety such as peanuts, cashews or almonds, alone or with raisins, sunflower seeds, pumpkin seeds

Peanut butter—stuffed into an apple or on celery sticks

Cottage cheese or cheese spread—in celery sticks or cucumber boats

Chicken or turkey—cubes, wings or drumsticks

Meat—in pieces, slices or cubes

Meatloaf slice

Hard-cooked eggs—shelled for the younger child

Yogurt

Most kids are quite happy to discover proteins such as luncheon meats, sliced ham and beef jerky in their lunch bags. However the label-reading parent quickly discovers that along with the protein these foods also contain nitrates, salt, preservatives, usually corn syrup and other sugars. What is not on the label is their high fat content. If you use them, think of them only as an occasional change of pace.

Remember to keep the normally refrigerated foods in the refrigerator until your child is leaving for school.

Peanut Butter Balls

½ cup (8 Tbsp.) peanut butter
½ cup honey (consider using
    part molasses)
2 Tbsp. powdered milk

1 cup toasted wheat germ
coconut (optional)

Mix ingredients well. Shape into balls, then roll in coconut (optional) or pat flat in a pan as for fudge. Refrigerate.

Variation: Press between two squares of Chex cereal.

Hot Lunch To Go

In a wide mouth thermal jug, add:

    A hefty soup
    Frankfurter in hot soup
    Macaroni and cheese
    Chili

You may wish to include a moist towelette as well as a napkin. (Or maybe both are wishful thinking!)

Sandwiches

Sandwiches are the versatile, flexible and traditional vehicle for providing protein rich foods. A sandwich is usually 60 percent bread, so it is important that you use a good bread. A good bread is made of enriched flour rather than plain white flour. A better bread is made of whole wheat or other whole grain flours.

Why is whole wheat flour in our bread important? Wheat, the basic ingredient in bread products, consists of a core encrusted in an outer brown covering called bran, and a small section known as the wheat germ. Towards the end of the 19th century, millers found that by changing from stone wheels to steel rollers, it was possible to inexpensively separate the outer covering of the wheat containing the bran and wheat germ from the kernel, leaving white flour. It made very light baked goods and had a very long shelf life. Most of the wheat's important value, however, is contained in the bran and the wheat germ. The bran covering provides fiber and bulk plus essential minerals and some vitamins. Wheat germ, besides being a good source of vitamin E and the vitamin B family, is high in protein, calcium, iron and phosphorous. Millers were not overly concerned that much of the nutritional benefits had been processed out because white flour was a commercial success.

In 1941 the United States government set standards for the enrichment of white flour that called for putting back of a dozen of the 22 nutrients that had been milled out. Those restored were put back in their level of strength present before refinement. They were thiamin, riboflavin, niacin and iron; but none of the other essential minerals and vitamins were replaced. So today we have enriched flour. While it certainly is better to buy enriched flour than flour not enriched, whole wheat flour is far more nutritious because *all* the "enrichment" is there naturally.

So, if you want the school sandwich to offer more per bite, whole wheat bread is the place to start. Your children don't like whole grain breads? Don't make the transition overnight. Start with a light whole grain bread which contains both whole wheat and enriched white flour. Experiment. Read labels carefully. Don't equate a dark bread with whole wheat. Often caramel coloring is used to give the appearance of whole wheat bread. Some parents use one side with white bread and one with whole wheat as their compromise. No need to announce the new plan. Work at it gradually unless going "cold turkey" is more effective for you. Kids will eat what is there, especially when they realize after a few days that they have no alternative.

There are other breads that can provide variety as well as good nutrition in your packed lunch. Don't forget about bagels, pita breads, croissants, small cocktail whole grain breads or English muffins.

In the following list of ideas, remember that the major protein value will come from what you put between the slices of bread and not from the bread itself.

Peanut Butter and (_____) Sandwiches

Peanut butter combines well with:

honey	sliced bananas
grated carrots	raisins
applesauce	bacon bits
cream cheese	jam/jelly
toasted wheat germ	cut-up dates

or any combination of the above

Peanut butter sandwiches freeze well and are easy to make ahead. They are especially easy to make on bread still frozen. Make a batch on Sunday night, or just make extras while you're preparing lunches some unhurried morning (*Good luck*!). In fact, buy an extra loaf for just this purpose. Make up the whole loaf (do not slice sandwiches), package in individual plastic bags and return them to the original plastic bag, and store in the freezer. Remove as needed—slice or not.

Variation: Peanut butter can also be spread on graham crackers as a thin sandwich.

Hint: Make your own "chunky style" peanut butter by adding sesame seeds and/or sunflower seeds that you've run briefly through the blender.

Yes, there are actually children who DO NOT LIKE peanut butter. No need to rush to your nearest psychiatrist! There are documented cases of normal development among such children.

Check page 120 for tips on what to look for when buying peanut butter.

Tuna Fish Sandwiches

Tuna fish and mayonnaise combine with:

pickle relish	sliced cucumbers
sunflower seeds	sprouts
sliced avocado	grated carrot
chopped celery	sliced egg

Mayonnaise in a sandwich does not hold up well without refrigeration. It turns rancid upon prolonged exposure to heat. Avoid using it for summer camp lunches, or if your child's lunch will be sitting on a radiator in school all morning. Mayonnaise usually does not freeze well. If the amount you are using in your sandwich mix is small, however, you should have no trouble keeping sandwiches mixed with mayonnaise in the freezer. This also holds true for egg salad that is well mashed.

Hint: Reduce the fat content of added mayonnaise by combining 2 parts low-fat plain yogurt with one part mayonnaise.

If you plan to add lettuce (and your child plans to eat it) you may wish to consider wrapping it separately in the lunch bag for placing in the sandwich just before it's to be eaten.

Cream Cheese Sandwiches

Cream cheese combines well with:

bacon bits	crushed pineapple
chopped nuts	luncheon meats
peanut butter	sliced egg
sliced cucumber	marmalade or jam
raisins—whole or ground	

Unlike most other cheese, cream cheese does not have a high protein value though it does have a high fat content. Don't get in the habit of spreading it on very thickly. Combining cream cheese with other protein foods will provide a more nutritious sandwich. Also, cream cheese spreads with greater success on sliced frozen bread.

Hint: One enrichment technique is to mix a tablespoon of powdered milk into an 8-ounce bar of cream cheese.

Variation: For a change, serve it on raisin bread or canned brown bread.

Do-It-Yourself Grape Jelly

Somewhere back in history, jelly became a must in both peanut butter and cream cheese sandwiches. If you have ever made jelly yourself you know that sugar is the major ingredient. In fact, so much sugar goes into making jellies and jams that you always need to buy extra. But here is a recipe for making you own grape jelly that, while not sugarless, contains far less sugar than is used in those commercial products. With this recipe you also eliminate the use of artificial colorings and flavorings.

Method #1

1 (12-oz.) can frozen grape juice concentrate
½ (1¾ oz.) pkg. of Slim Set™ Jelling Mix

Add one half of the Slim Set™ box contents to the thawed frozen grape juice concentrate. Heat to boiling. Simmer together for one minute, then remove from heat to cool. Pour into a wide mouth jar and refrigerate.

Slim Set™ is a jelling mix that jells liquids without the aid of added sugar. It is usually found in the grocery section with canning supplies.

Method #2

1 (12 oz.) can frozen grape juice concentrate
1 envelope unflavored gelatin

Dissolve the gelatin in the defrosted juice concentrate. Pour the mixture into a saucepan and heat to boiling or until the gelatin dissolves. Remove from heat, cool slightly, then pour into a wide mouth jar. Refrigerate.

This jelly does not spread as easily as the first method, but it still works well.

To make a completely sugarless jelly, use frozen apple juice concentrate or Seneca frozen grape juice concentrate. Be sure to check content labels for added sugar.

Sandwich Spreads

Here's hoping you have some tried-and-true spread recipes that your children like. I have only two! The major advantage of the first one is that it requires opening only one jar when preparing a sandwich— a small but significant point.

Peanut-Butter-Like-No-Other

Combine:

1 cup (16 Tbsp.) peanut butter
¼ cup powdered milk
2½ Tbsp. honey
½ cup toasted wheat germ
½ mashed banana

Home-Made Cheese Whiz

(Great for sandwiches, snacks and traveling too!)

2 Tbsp. butter or margarine	1 (13 oz.) can of evaporated
1½ lbs. American processed	milk
cheese	1 Tbsp. flour
2 egg yolks, beaten	

In a double boiler, melt butter and add cheese. When softened, add egg yolks, milk and flour. Cook until thick. Store in a covered jar in the refrigerator.

Hint: Use this melted over cooked macaroni.

And, one last sandwich reminder, sliced turkey from the deli counter is a good low-fat protein that children usually enjoy…and eat!

A Fruit or Vegetable

The obvious:

pickles	green pepper strips
cherry tomatoes	celery
carrot sticks	cucumber slices
peaches	seedless grapes
bananas	oranges (quartered)
apples	dried fruit

Hint: An apple can be cored, halved and placed back together to minimize browning. Any cut fruits, such as apples and peaches, can be prevented from turning brown by putting lemon, orange, or grapefruit juice on the cut sections.

A Make Ahead Idea: Slice several clean carrots into sticks and wrap in a dampened paper towel and store in a plastic bag to prevent them from drying out.

The not-so-obvious:

mandarin orange sections	pineapple in container
small salad in container	green or black olives
Chinese pea pods (which,	applesauce in container
when packed frozen, will	melon pieces cubed
defrost by lunch time)	

Hint: For disposable containers, use a glass baby food jar, a paper cup covered with foil or with a plastic bag twist-tied around it or even a plain plastic bag that closes well. Include a toothpick or a plastic spoon as disposable utensils.

Individual packaged foods may be more costly but losing plastic containers and your time to repackage foods from uneconomically sized packages adds up too. Well worth it are the single serving containers of applesauce and the occasional inclusions of the highly sugared (unfortunately) fruits such as diced peaches.

Speaking of paper goods, yes, remember to pack a paper napkin or section of paper towel. You should also save those little packets of ketchup, mustard, honey, and bread sticks that often accompany take-out food as they make good lunch box additions. This is also true for those packed-in-foil moist towelettes for cleanup.

Something Special

That something special—the treat that most kids look for first in their lunch pack—can be both good tasting and good for them.

Try:

raisins (bagged or boxed)
pretzels
granola bars
cheese and crackers package
carob-covered raisins
trail mix (gorp)
box of animal crackers
a fortune cookie
Graham crackers
Oatmeal cookies

popcorn in a bag
container of yogurt
sunflower seeds
Finger Jell-O™
cookies with "redeeming
   value" such as:
   Nutter-Butters
   Fig Newtons,
   Apple Newtons,
   Blueberry Newtons

If you're including some good homemade cookies, make them extra large when you bake. You'll find that one large cookie instead of two small ones has far more kid-appeal. (See page 66.)

Hint: Slice up any of your favorite dessert breads or cakes into individual portions, wrap well and freeze. Toss one into a lunch bag as needed. This is a good way to keep from eating up the leftovers yourself.

If your children understand that it's because you love them that you are not including Twinkies, they will feel special in a positive way among their sugar-consuming peers. Really! (And, boy, did my son ever crave Twinkies!)

Beverages

Milk
Apple juice (hot or cold)
Orange juice
Hot tea (weak) with orange juice
Juice drinks

Most schools provide milk or a drink for a nominal fee. Because of a government subsidy, your child can buy milk in school cheaper than you can provide it. If your child is "pocket-less" or forgetful, tape the milk money to the inside of the lunch box with masking tape.

A small box or can of fruit juice makes a good pack-along drink, although it is expensive on a per serving basis. Freeze the can or box before sending it off in the lunch bag. It will defrost in time for lunch and still be chilled. Box drinks are all too often the flavored water variety. Invest in your child's future health and buy the more expensive juice boxes.

Good drinks to include in a thermos are orange or apple juice. Hot soup is especially nice on a cold, wintry day. An occasional cooked hot dog carried in soup can be transferred at lunchtime to a bun, also provided in the lunch pack, and be a truly hot hot dog.

Food For Thought

On special occasions—or whenever you feel like doing something special, include a note (such as, "You're terrific," or "I love you," or "Happy Birthday"), a funny drawing, or a little toy or game. Egos need nourishment too!

And as a little food for thought for you, mom, keep in mind that a five-year-old and up, can assemble his or her own lunch bag with wrapped ahead "makings." Kids who are involved in the responsibility of making their own school lunches may well surprise you with their willingness and creativity. Either you or they can pack up the brown bag the night before and store it in the refrigerator so as to avoid the morning rush.

Bringing Treats to School

Before long, even though you are not a homeroom mother, you will need to supply a treat for the WHOLE class for a birthday, a festive occasion, or just because it's your turn. So what will be both appropriate and nutritious?

Snacks really fall into different categories. Banana slices dipped in honey and rolled in toasted wheat germ just don't make it as a child's birthday treat. Let's start with the good-and-fun school snack ideas that will serve 25 to 30 and leave the party ideas till the end.

Fruit Treats:

orange slices (circular slices are more fun)
apple slices spread with peanut butter
fruit and cheese kabobs—canned and/or fresh on toothpicks
bananas for children to slice and serve
dried apricots (2 bags)

Crunchy Treats:

These should be prepackaged in individual plastic bags or bring small paper cups as serving containers:

granola (store bought or homemade)
popcorn (store bought or homemade)
"Cruncho" (page 42)

Hint: You will need 2 (16 oz.) boxes of granola to serve 25 to 30 children.

Other Treat Ideas:

Yummie Balls (page 45)
Finger Jell-O™ (page 46), double this recipe
large soft pretzels (page 49)
carrot sticks served with a dip (if setting is appropriate)
celery filled with peanut butter or cream cheese with
     raisins (traditionally known as "Ants on a Log")
quartered peanut butter, open face sandwiches

or...

Egg Sailboats

1 doz. eggs, hard-cooked   2 doz. toothpicks
½ cup mayonnaise   one sheet of paper
1 tsp. mustard

Shell eggs, slice in half and remove yolks. Combine yolks with mayonnaise and mustard and return a spoonful of mixture to the hollow of each egg white. Tape small paper triangles to toothpicks (or let your child do that part) and stick them in egg halves prior to serving.

School Time Drinks

Providing a good tasting, good-for-you, affordable drink for a class-room is not easy. The obviously convenient and economical drinks (such as Hi-C, Tang, Kool-Aid) are usually rejected by those wishing to stay away from artificial colorings and flavorings and provide a better food value drink. Access to refrigeration can also influence drink choices. The choice selection is really not very wide if you wish to avoid added sugars and artificial sweeteners and have a limited budget.

milk
frozen juice concentrates, reconstituted
unsweetened apple juice—a gallon container or frozen
     concentrate variety
ice water

Today's selection of boxes of liquid juice concentrate (especially in the cranberry juice family) work very well in these situations.

Party Favors

If you're not planning on bringing a food treat to mark the occasion of that highest of days—your child's birthday—a birthday favor can mark the occasion.

For each child, one or a combination of the following:

     a balloon (always a hit!)
     a piece of sugarless gum, individually wrapped

a pack of sugarless gum, if your budget allows
a novelty pencil or eraser
a new comb (from an inexpensive combination package)
a 6" ruler
a sticker or decal

But if food it must be, try:

Candy Cookies

(*This recipe makes a large-size, heavily sugared but very popular cookie.*)

1 cup liquid corn oil
1 cup brown sugar
½ cup white sugar
2 eggs, beaten
2 tsp. vanilla

1½ tsp. baking soda
2¼ cups flour (white, or half
    white and half whole wheat)
1 cup (or less) "M&M's" Plain
    Chocolate Candies

Combine oil, sugars, eggs and vanilla. Mix dry ingredients together and combine with creamed mixture. Drop by the teaspoonful onto an ungreased cookie sheet. Flatten to not more than 2 inches in diameter. Decorate with 3-5 candies per cookie, half pressing them into the dough. IT IS IMPERATIVE THAT THE NUMBER OF CANDIES BE THE SAME FOR EACH COOKIE. Bake at 375° for 8-10 minutes. It is common for the candies to crack. This recipe makes 2-4 dozen cookies depending on the size of your teaspoon.

Hint: Be sure to use the Cornell Triple Rich formula when making these cookies to ease your conscience. (See page 124.)

Party Popcorn

While the number of marshmallows in this recipe does tend to boggle the mind, I rationalize their use by the inclusion of nuts and sunflower seeds.

10 cups popped popcorn
¼ cup (½ stick) margarine or
    butter
1 (10 oz.) bag of
    marshmallows

½ cup sunflower seeds
1 cup nuts
½ cup (8 Tbsp.) peanut butter
    (optional)

Melt the shortening in a 3-quart saucepan. Add marshmallows and cook over low heat till syrupy. Remove from heat. Add peanut butter, if using. Add popcorn, seeds and nuts, and stir till they are well coated.

Variations:

- With buttered hands, form into balls and place in cupcake papers.

- Fill 20 to 25 (5 oz.) paper cups half full and add a popsicle stick for a handle. After cooled and hardened, run knife around inside of cup to loosen.

- Spread in a large shallow greased pan and press down with a spatula or wax paper. When cool, cut into bars. If you want larger bars, you will need to make two batches.

Hint: These balls, pops or bars can be perked up futher with raisins, sprinkles or candles. Food colorings can be added to the "syrup" before adding the popcorn.

Aggression Cookies

This time-honored classic oatmeal cookie can be enriched by using whole wheat flour in combination with white and it still tastes terrific.

Combine:

3 cups brown sugar
3 cups (6 sticks) butter or
    margarine (or any
    combination of the two)
1 tsp. vanilla

3 cups flour (white, whole
    wheat or half and half)
1 Tbsp. baking soda
6 cups oatmeal, uncooked

There is only one way to mix this and that is to use your hands and any other hands you can enlist. Knead until there aren't any lumps of butter. Roll the dough into small balls and place them on an ungreased cookie sheet. Flatten gently with a small fork. Bake 10-12 minutes at 350°. Cool before removing from cookie sheet. This recipe makes between 10 and 15 dozen cookies, enough to serve two homeroom classes and still leave some for home snacks. If you have room, store some in your freezer.

If you're up to making a cake, try the chocolate cake recipe on page 68. It will make a large, low pan cake or two dozen cupcakes which you can then frost.

If you are bringing homemade cookies, top off a nutritious cookie with a smile face made by squeezing homemade frosting from the corner of a small plastic bag—*corner snipped off, of course!*

Some schools do not allow homemade treats to be served in the classroom. About the only alternative you have is to select such items as peanut butter cookies, oatmeal cookies, gingerbread, lady fingers or carrot cake from your local bakery or grocery store. Or if your budget allows, individual boxes of animal crackers or Cracker Jacks are always a big hit!

Your School's Lunch Program

The school lunch program, which you may or may not be using, is under scrutiny. An annual $400 million of wasted, uneaten food alarmed both Congress and the Department of Agriculture, which administers the national school lunch program. All children are served standard portions despite different appetites and food preferences. Now elementary schools have the option that was once reserved for only the upper grades. The "offer versus serve" decision made at the school district level, allows children to choose 3 out of 5 components offered at lunch.

Have lunch with your child at school one day to check the quality and the atmosphere. If you are interested in improving your school's lunch program, contact Sara Sloan for information by sending her a self-addressed stamped envelope or order her *SCHOOL KIT* which contains 2 tape cassettes about how to get nutrition served at school, and weaning your child from junk food. Included also is the booklet, How to Get Healthy School Meals, plus resource sheets and articles, all for $14.95 ppd. This is available from Nutra, PO Box 13825, Atlanta, GA 30325 (404) 634-5264.

Try Recess First

Certain schools have broken the tradition of lunch first, then recess. They have discovered that by letting children play first and then eat, that children don't feel rushed to finish (or not finish) lunch and there is less plate waste. It is an idea you might like to discuss with your school administrator or PTA. It does present a school with scheduling problems but the end result is worth it, most say.

Tasty Alternatives to Junk Food Snacks

Many children, mine included, seem to snack all day long. This is not necessarily a bad thing. Many parents act as though one of the Ten Commandments reads, "*Thou shalt eat three meals a day*," but little children don't follow rules all that well. If their snacks are nutritious, and they are not snacking too close to mealtime (make a "Kitchen Closed" sign you can display an hour before mealtime), snacking should not be a problem. Perhaps if you view snacks as mini-meals (but not crying or knee-injury solace) they will be easier to accept.

The experts are also coming up with studies which show that several mini-meals are more healthful for you. Snacking doesn't produce overweight problems—it's what you learn to snack on.

Regrettably, snacks are often things that come out of boxes and bags in the forms of candy and chips. They supply energy but not essential nutrients. They are often too salty, sugary or fatty processed foods. The challenge lies in trying to switch children from snacks with lesser food value to more wholesome ones.

Our society believes (thanks to advertising by the sugar industry) that sugared treats are a better pick-me-up than protein-packed snacks. Untrue! Not only are protein snacks—pieces of cheese, for example—a more beneficial pick-me-up, but they continue their good work by staying with you longer and contributing to growing strong, healthy bodies.

It's almost un-American to deny children snacks of candy or chips, especially when they are snacking at someone else's house. In your own home, though, you can go a long way toward correcting the "candy is dandy" image. The best technique is NOT TO HAVE IT IN THE HOUSE. If you believe that your kids are really eating too many unnecessary foods, don't buy them!

More and more parents who restrict their small children's exposure to sugared and/or salty treats tell me that their children don't seem to crave or request them. They report that their children's tastes adapt until they find candy, salted chips and crackers too difficult to finish.

Adults I've met whose parents were nutrition-conscious often carry their parents' concern into adulthood. They look back, grateful to their parents, admitting at the same time they were not so grateful as children.

It is hard for a child—anyone, for that matter—to understand that what tastes so good is not necessarily good for you. One theory on why sweets are so appealing is based on the fact that human beings cannot make their own vitamin C, but must consume it. Vitamin C occurs naturally in citrus fruits, some vegetables (green peppers, for one), berries and leaves—foods which also have a sweet taste. Through evolution our taste buds may have guided us to foods which were sweet because they were good for us, but white refined sugar (not a naturally occurring food) contains no vitamin C, yet we consume it as though our lives depended on it.

What do you do about the child who walks into your house carrying candy, or when your child goes next door and is offered a sugary treat? You can realistically concern yourself only with what is brought into your house and not worry about what is eaten at a neighbor's.

When sweets are brought into our house, I allow one taste, then remove them to a secure place until it is time for the guest to take them home. If you are confident that sweets are not a basic part of your child's diet, you can probably do more harm than good by making them forbidden food outside the home.

I resent most TV commercials that equate sugar and empty calories with parental love. Real love for your children should encourage you to restrict refined sugars and refined flours, salt, fats, artificial colorings and flavorings in an effort to improve their health in mind and body. Tell your children that the reason you don't want them to eat these extraneous foods is BECAUSE YOU LOVE THEM and you want them to be strong and healthy. They might not always like the answer but they will understand it and won't stop loving you.

Some general good snack guidelines:

- Set a good example yourself.
- Don't use food as a pacifer, punishment or prize.
- Take the time to have homemade snacks easily available.
- Serve snacks attractively so they are interesting to eat.
- Introduce a new food as a snack when your child is hungriest.

By developing a snack knack, you can help fill the diet voids of any picky eater or nibbler you might have in your house.

We don't always have to be creative to make good snacks for the after school crowd. Some lightly buttered whole wheat toast with or without a bit of sugared cinnamon on it, or even a peanut butter sandwich quartered, will be happily devoured.

Here are some good tasting snack ideas I'd like to share. Some are sugar-free, some are not. Most contain no salt. Recipes that do contain sugar have been selected because they include other nutritious ingredients which give them redeeming value. Honey, because of its cost, is not always a practical substitute for white sugar. Variety, not sugar or salt, is the spice of life. And moderation in all things. Much as I would prefer to live in a world in which sugar and other additives to our food supply were healthful, that is just not the case.

Frozen Snacks

The following popsicle recipes don't specify paper cup size or popsicle mold size. Only you know the amount your child can consume in one sitting with minimum drip.

Frozen Banana Rockets

1 banana
2 popsicle sticks
honey and toasted wheat germ or chopped nuts
peanut butter (optional)

Peel one firm, ripe banana. Cut in half, or even thirds. Insert one stick lengthwise through the center of each section. Wrap in plastic and place in the freezer. When ready to eat, dip in honey, (or smush with peanut butter) and roll in toasted wheat germ or chopped nuts.

Hint: Frozen bananas are good without being dipped in anything!

Variation: Yes, you can also dip them in melted chocolate chips, but why bother?

Orange Juice-Sicles

1 (6 oz.) can frozen orange juice
3 cans cold water
1 egg white

2 Tbsp. sweetner (sugar, honey or artificial sweetener)
popsicle sticks and cups

Mix in blender. Pour into molds, insert sticks and freeze.

Variety Pack Popsicles

1 (6 oz.) can frozen orange juice concentrate, softened
    (or use grape juice, cranberry juice or Hawaiian Punch)
1 (6 oz.) can water
1 pt. vanilla ice cream, softened (or two containers of
    plain yogurt)
popsicle sticks and cups

Whir in a blender. Pour into molds, insert sticks, and freeze.

Polynesian Popsicles

1 cup skim milk
1 envelope unflavored gelatin
½ cup sugar or honey
1 egg white

1¼ cups apricot nectar or
   canned pineapple juice
popsicle sticks and cups

Pour milk into blender and add gelatin. Let soften for one minute before adding the rest of the ingredients to whip. Pour into molds, insert sticks and freeze.

Creamsicles

1 (6 oz.) can peaches in light
   syrup or 2 fresh ripe
   peaches, sliced or pitted
1 cup heavy cream

1 tsp. sugar or honey
   (optional)
popsicle sticks and cups

Whip cream in a blender for 30-45 seconds. Add peaches and honey. Whir until smooth. Pour into molds, insert sticks and freeze.

Chocolate Pops

1 (8 oz.) container plain
   yogurt
2 Tbsp. cocoa or carob
   powder

2 Tbsp. brown sugar or honey
popsicle sticks and cups

Liquify in a blender, pour into molds, insert popsicle sticks and freeze.

Snow Cones

Crush several ice cubes with ½ cup water in a blender, turning it on and off to achieve a snowy consistency. Pour over the "snow," which has been scooped into paper cups, either:

2 Tbsp. thawed frozen juice or concentrate

or

2 Tbsp. warmed honey to which food coloring has been added.

Keep-on-Hand Snow Cones

Freeze orange juice (or any other flavored juice) in ice cube trays. Pop frozen juice cubes into a plastic bag to store. Put three to six of these cubes at a time in a blender. Turn blender on and off until cubes reach snowy consistency. Pile into a paper cup to serve.

The whole batch blended at once will keep its carnival consistency stored in a container in the freezer. Kids can serve themselves. Adding a little water makes it a "slush." Even kids who don't usually care for orange juice like it this way.

Watermelon Popsicles

1 cup seedless watermelon
   chunks
1 cup orange juice

1 cup water
popsicle sticks and cups

Blend these ingredients in a blender, pour into molds, insert sticks and freeze.

Frozen Veggies

Offer your child a small paper cupful of frozen peas or frozen corn right from the package. Chinese pea pods frozen are also a favorite of some.

Variation: For a change of pace, serve frozen seedless grapes. Freeze them first on a shallow tray after they are washed and separated. When stored in a large bag, they will then not stick together.

Dippy Snacks

With carrots, celery, green pepper strips, cucumber slices, cherry tomatoes, cauliflower pieces or crackers, try any of the following:

Cheese Spread

1 stick (½ cup) butter or margarine, softened
1 cup cottage cheese
garlic powder

Blend shortening with cottage cheese. A blender or baby food grinder will give you a smoother consistency than whipping with a fork. Add garlic powder to taste. Refrigerate in a covered container.

Dip It Again

1 (8 oz.) container of plain yogurt
1 cup sour cream
1 pkg. onion soup mix

Combine and chill before serving.

Better-With-Buttermilk Dip

1 cup buttermilk
2 cups mayonnaise
1 cup sour cream or yogurt

1 envelope Ranch style
   salad dressing mix

Stir together and chill. For use as salad dressing, substitute a second cup of buttermilk for the sour cream or yogurt.

Hint: Use cucumber "coins" in place of crackers.

Other *quickie dippies* that make up in small quantities are:

- Blend ⅓ to ½ of a mashed banana with 2 or 3 tsps. of mayonnaise.

- Whip together 1 tsp. of smooth peanut butter with 1 tsp. of mayonnaise. If still too thick, add a few drops of milk.

- Mix ½ tsp. of lemon juice and ½ tsp. of honey or sugar to 1 or 2 tsp. of mayonnaise.

Cutting Up With Kids

Have your children help you cut up green onions, parsley, lettuce, cheese slices, fruit, etc. using a scissors instead of a knife. Using a scissors helps coordination, and keeps them busy for a *long* time!

Cherry Balls

Stuff whole (or half) cherry tomatoes with cream cheese, a cheese spread, egg salad or tuna salad.

Actually thinking of snacks as hors d'oeuvres—rather than desserts—will open up a whole new way of looking at this category.

Crunchy Snacks

Have you thought of putting crackers in your cookie jar? They are made with less sugar and you can choose a low salt variety. You can fill a cookie jar with peanuts-in-the-shell or roasted no-salt nuts. Or keep on hand a jar of nuts and raisins with a few chocolate chips thrown in (aka "Gorp").

Popcorn

Of all the gadgets available to us today the electric hot air popper is probably one of the best you can buy from a nutritional snack point-of-view. Popcorn is good tasting, fun to make and a popular sugar-free food. It is low in calories, at least until you add coatings. It is also a good source of fiber. Hot-air popper and microwave popcorn dishes allow you to pop corn without using any additional fats.

In addition to a bit of melted butter, try sprinkling grated Parmesan or American cheese on popcorn. Or mix with peanuts; or cinnamon.

Package extra popcorn in small plastic bags with twist ties—excellent for an out-of-doors treat, car ride or TV special snack.

Honey "Cracker Jacks"

½ cup (8 Tbsp.) honey   6 cups popped corn
¼ cup butter or margarine   1 cup shelled peanuts

Heat honey and butter in a saucepan until blended. Cool. Pour over popcorn which has been mixed with peanuts, stirring as you pour. When well-coated, spread in a pan in a single layer. Bake at 350° 5-10 minutes or until crisp, stirring several times. The difference between crisp (not brown) and burnt can be a matter of minutes. Package in plastic bags and twist-tie. If you want it to be mistaken for the "real thing," add a small toy.

Variation: Food coloring added to honey gives a festive appearance.

Commercial Cracker Jacks, though sugar-coated, contain no artificial colorings or flavorings and are mainly popcorn. They make a nice change-of-pace and easy to have on hand snack.

Popcorn Candy Clusters

1 cup (8 oz.) semi-sweet chocolate chips
1 cup freshly popped popcorn
1 cup nuts

Melt chocolate chips. Add popcorn and nuts and stir until they are well coated. Drop by spoonfuls onto a cookie sheet or wax paper and let set till firm. If the crowd is rushing you for a taste, chill the clusters in the freezer for 5 minutes. When firm, store in plastic bags.

Cruncho Mix

Mix:

4 cups crunchy cereal (such as Cheerios or Corn Chex or any combination)
1 cup peanuts or mixed nuts
1 cup pretzel sticks, the smallest size
1 cup seasoned croutons

Combine:

½ cup salad oil or 6 Tbsp. melted butter
2 tsp. Worcestershire Sauce
¼ tsp. garlic powder

In a large shallow pan coat crunchy ingredients with the combined oil and seasonings. Heat in oven at 250° for about 45 minutes, stirring every 15 minutes. Spread on absorbent paper to cool.

Granola Bars

½ cup light corn syrup
⅔ cup (10 Tbsp.) peanut
    butter

1 carrot grated (optional)
3 cups granola (bought or
    homemade)

Butter a 9-inch square pan. In a 3-quart saucepan boil corn syrup for 1 minute only, stirring constantly. Remove from heat. Stir in peanut butter. Stir in granola, and grated carrot if using. Work fast as it hardens quickly. Transfer to pan. Spread and pat in place with a spoon or dampened spatula. Cool for an hour before cutting into bars.

Great Gorpies

2 sticks (1 cup) butter or
    margarine
1 handful each of
    raisins
    peanuts
    chocolate chips

1 cup brown sugar
2 cups flour (white or half
    white, half whole wheat)
1 tsp. baking soda
2 tsp. milk

Cream shortening and sugar until smooth. Add all the handfuls, going heavier on the first two and lighter on the chocolate chips. Mix well, then add combined flour and baking soda. Add milk. Drop by tablespoons on a greased cookie sheet. Bake at 350° about 10 minutes or until done. Leave on cookie sheet a minute or two before lifting them off, as they might crumble. Makes 3 dozen cookies.

Hint: If an adult is measuring out the handfuls of peanuts, raisins and chocolate chips, use only one handful of each; if a child is measuring, use two or three handfuls.

Grape Granola Bars

½ cup butterscotch chips
⅔ cups grape jelly
2 cups granola

1 cup oatmeal (uncooked)
½ cup peanuts

Melt butterscotch chips over low heat, stirring constantly. Add jelly and stir till blended. Remove from heat. Add granola, oatmeal and chopped peanuts. Mix till well coated. Spread in a buttered 9-inch square pan. Refrigerate until firm. Cut into bars.

Breakfast Granola Bars

(*They hold together well and are so-o-o easy!*)

2 cups granola
2 eggs, beaten
dash of vanilla for sweetening (optional)

Combine the granola and eggs in a greased 8-inch square pan. Bake at 350° for 15 minutes. Cut into 8 bars. When serving spread with jam, honey or peanut butter.

Peanut-Butter-Bear-Bars

1 loaf of sliced bread,
   preferably whole wheat
1 pkg. peanuts, chopped
peanut oil

1 cup peanut butter
¼ cup toasted wheat germ
   (optional)

Trim crusts from bread. Halve slices. Dry bread and crusts on a cookie sheet overnight in your oven, or in the oven at 150° for half an hour. Crumb dry crusts in a blender. Combine crust crumbs with chopped nuts and wheat germ, if using. Thin peanut butter with oil. Spread with, or dip the bread in, the thinned peanut butter, then roll it in the nut/crumb mixture. Store in an airtight container.

Variation: Add Tbsp. of cocoa or carob powder to the thinned peanut butter.

Quickie Cookies A La Stove Top

1 cup sugar
¼ cup (½ stick) butter or
   margarine
½ tsp. vanilla
2 Tbsp. cocoa

¼ cup milk
1½ cups oatmeal, uncooked
½ cup toasted wheat germ
¼ cup (8 Tbsp.) peanut butter

Combine sugar, cocoa, butter and milk in a saucepan and boil over medium heat for 1 minute. Stirring constantly, fold in remaining ingredients. Drop with a teaspoon on wax paper and let harden. Work quickly because the hardening doesn't take long. Store in an airtight container because they can also dry out.

Crunchies

½ cup butter or margarine
¼ cup (4 Tbsp.) honey
¼ cup sugar

4 cups oatmeal, uncooked
1 cup raisins (optional)

Melt shortening. Add honey and sugar. Add oatmeal (and raisins) quickly before sugar dissolves completely. Blend well and press into a buttered 9 x 13 inch pan. Bake at 400° for 8-10 minutes. Cut into squares while still slightly warm but don't remove from pan until they are firm.

Variation: Dribble ¾ cup or less of melted chocolate chips over Crunchies while they are still warm.

No-Bake Dateballs

¾ cup brown sugar
2 eggs, beaten
1 cup dates, cut up
1 cup chopped nuts
1 tsp. vanilla

2 cups cereal (1 cup each of
any of the following: Rice
Krispies, granola or
puffed cereal)
coconut (optional)

In a two-quart saucepan mix sugar, eggs and dates. Stir over medium heat about 5 minutes or until mixture pulls away from the pan. Cook 3 minutes longer. Remove from heat and add vanilla and nuts. Fold in cereal. Butter fingers to form mixture into balls. Roll balls in coconut if desired. Let cool. Store in an airtight container.

Yummie Balls

Combine:

½ cup (8 Tbsp.) peanut butter
½ cup (8 Tbsp.) honey
½ cup cocoa or carob powder
1 cup toasted wheat germ

1 cup peanuts or soy nuts
(chopped if preferred)
½ cup sunflower seeds
coconut (optional)

Roll into balls and roll in coconut. Refrigerate if using a refrigerated brand of peanut butter, which would be preferable.

Ants on a Log

Stuff celery stick with cream cheese or peanut butter and dot with raisins.

Variation: Turn these into "hot rods" by putting toothpicks through the front and back ends and placing carrot circle slices on the ends of the toothpicks for wheels.

Swords

Banana slices, cheese slices, and cherry tomatoes can be "speared" on thin pretzel sticks.

Just Plain Good

Magic Finger Jell-O™, the kind that disappears before your very eyes, is an all-time favorite of kids. If you want it without artificial flavorings and colorings, try the next recipe. If you want it without artificial flavorings and colorings and without SUGAR, try Apple Finger Jell-O™.

Grape Finger Jell-O™

1 (12 oz.) can frozen grape juice concentrate, thawed
3 envelopes unflavored gelatin
1½ cups (1 can) water

Soften gelatin in grape juice. Boil the water, add the juice/gelatin mixture and stir till gelatin dissolves. Remove from heat, pour into a lightly greased 9 x 13-inch pan and chill. Cut into squares when firm. Refrigerate in a covered container. This is good lunch box and traveling fare. It can go unrefrigerated for 4 hours under normal conditions.

Variation: You can substitute frozen cranberry juice cocktail concentrate for grape juice.

Apple Finger Jell-O™

1 (12 oz.) can frozen apple (or pear/apple) juice
    concentrate, thawed
3 envelopes unflavored gelatin
1½ cups (1 can) water

Follow directions for Grape Finger Jell-O™.

Variation: By using only 2 envelopes of unflavored gelatin you can make regular Apple Jell-O™.

If you have 2 bananas on hand, one fun way of serving this extra firm gelatin snack is as:

Slippery Circles

Let any of the above recipes for Finger Jell-O™ stand and chill till thickened, which doesn't take very long (15 to 25 minutes). Place a spoonful of the gelatin into each of 4 empty and clean 6 oz. cans, such as usually used for frozen orange juice. Cut a peeled banana in half and center it in the can. Spoon in remaining gelatin. Chill till firm. To unmold, dip to rim in warm water and let it slide out. Or remove bottom of can if more appropriate. Cut in slices.

Sunshine Squares

(*A Finger Jell-O™ that is good even for breakfast!*)

4 envelopes unflavored
   gelatin
¾ cup pineapple juice
1 cup boiling water

¼ cup sugar
1 cup orange juice

Soften gelatin in pineapple juice. Add to boiling water and stir until dissolved. Add sweetener and orange juice. Chill in a 9 x 9-inch pan, then cut into squares. Refrigerate in a covered container.

Variation: If you wish to use honey instead of sugar, decrease the orange juice by ⅛ of a cup.

Apple Ring Snacks

Why pay for Weight Watcher's Apple Snack when you can make your own?

Peel an apple and remove the core. Slice in rings. Place on a lightly greased cookie sheet, or on clear plastic wrap laid out on a cookie sheet. Dry in an electric oven at low or warm temperature; in a gas oven the pilot light is sufficient. Drying takes 6-9 hours, making this a good overnight project. The size of the apple slices and your oven temperature are the variables you will have to experiment with. The apples need not be dried to a crisp. Store in an airtight container. These should last several weeks at room temperature. Good for traveling!

Fruit Leather

Use apples, peaches, pears or nectarines to make this yummy dried "candy" that is more nutritious than what you would be buying at the store.

This is a good way to use up fruits otherwise unedible. This recipe works on canned fruit which is well drained. Use mashed or pureed fruit.

Two methods work well. FIRST is the blender way. Peel and core fruit, blend till smooth, then cook 5 minutes in sauce pan over moderate heat. SECOND is the freeze-defrost method. In advance, peel and core fruit and place it wrapped in the freezer. Remove from freezer a hour before using so it can start to defrost. Cook in a saucepan, mashing with fork as you go. Cook for 5-10 minutes. If very watery, drain. While cooking add 1 tsp. honey for each piece of fruit you are using. (Cook the different fruits separately, though you can cook 1 piece or a dozen of the same type at one time.)

Lay out clear plastic wrap (or cut open small plastic bags) on a cookie sheet or broiling tray. Use one piece for each piece of fruit you have cooked. Spoon mixture onto the wrap staying away from its edge. Spread as thin as possible. If you spread another piece of plastic wrap over the mixture and press down with a wide spatula, it helps to make it evenly thin. Be sure to remove this top sheet of plastic before drying.

Place your tray in the oven (at night, we suggest) which is turned on to its lowest possible heat or with just the pilot light on, and leave overnight (6-8 hours). The plastic wrap will not melt! If it is dry by breakfast, remove from the oven (if not, wait a while longer) and roll up the plastic wrap (with the dried fruit) as if it were a jelly roll.

THEN—PEEL AND EAT!

It will last several months this way—if your children don't discover it, that is.

Fruit Cones

sliced strawberries	blueberries
small cubes of melon	grapes
mandarin orange sections	flat bottom ice cream cone

Fill as many cones as needed with any one or combination of the above fruits. Good going-outside snacks for one or a group.

Soft Wholewheat Pretzels

2 (16 oz.) loaves frozen whole
    wheat bread dough,
    thawed

1 egg white, slightly beaten
1 tsp. water
coarse salt (optional)

Thaw bread in the refrigerator overnight. From each loaf shape 12 1½ inch balls. Roll each ball into a rope approximately 14 inches long. Shape into pretzels by forming a knot and looping ends through. Arrange pretzels one inch apart on well-greased baking sheet. Let stand for 20 minutes. Brush combined egg white and water on pretzels, then sprinkle with coarse salt. Place a shallow pan containing one inch of boiling water on a lower rack in the oven. Bake pretzels on a cookie sheet on a rack above the water at 350° for 20 minutes or till golden brown. Makes two dozen pretzels.

Variation 1: Pretzel sticks can be made by beginning with balls rolled into 8 inch sticks. Try pretzel letters, which is something your children will enjoy helping you do.

Variation 2: Roll sticks 4-6 inches long in a mixture of melted butter, cinnamon and sugar before baking.

Snack Drinks

We tend to forget that the drinks we rely on to satisfy our thirst also provide many calories. Drinks, therefore, do qualify as snacks.

I have read that we drink 42 gallons of soft drinks a year per person. The average can of regular soda has approximately 9 to 10 teaspoons of sugar. That's where we consume most of our added caloric sweeteners. While diet sodas offer sweetness without calories, the whole question of artificial sweeteners and the amounts we are now consuming, is another controversial additive topic. Aspartame, marketed as NutraSweet, is 180 times sweeter than sugar and is now used in more than 70 products but mainly in sugar-free drinks. While the American Medical Association has issued a statement that aspartame is safe for most people, not everyone agrees. It has been recommended that we don't consume more than 22 milligrams of aspartame per one pound of body weight per day. That translates to not more than 14 cans of soda with NutraSweet for the average adult. For a 30 pound child, however, that means not more than 4 cans.

Water

While not a snack, water—the original thirst quencher, must get top billing. It is essential and it is calorie-free! In recent history it has lost popularity to its competitors but water does have a value beyond washing dishes and flushing toilets. Not only is it vital to our body functions, it is readily available and CHEAP. Remember that water has been the number one drink for thousands of years. Soda did not travel on covered wagons. If you want your water to seem more appetizing, keep it cold in a nice container in the refrigerator. A young child may be enticed to drink water from his or her own container, small enough for safe pouring, or from a jug with a spigot. Plastic cups in a lower drawer encourage self-help and can save you many "*I'm thirsty*" trips.

Orange Juice

Orange juice is an excellent drink because it is both reasonably inexpensive and naturally sweet. Don't just relegate orange juice to morning breakfast. It is a terrific drink all day long. It is also a good idea to supplement orange juice with oranges themselves. The pulp and the meat of the orange have important nutrients that are missing from frozen concentrate.

Variation: Dilute orange juice with a clear soda like 7-Up® or seltzer to make your own orange soda.

Milk

Milk is a terrific food—yes, FOOD. Most health spokesmen today recommend drinking skim milk from age two since we seem to get enough fats elsewhere in our diet. The only difference between skim milk and regular milk is the fat content. Milk provides a good supply of vitamins A and D which you might not be getting elsewhere in your diet. Milk is also a major source of protein as well as calcium for growing children. If your child has an aversion to milk, however, and even the addition of carob powder or cocoa won't change his or her mind, do not despair. Cheese, yogurt, cottage cheese and even quality ice cream are good substitutes. Dark greens are also a good source of calcium. Powdered milk is an excellent method for sneaking in extra milk value as it can be added to many foods including cookies, scrambled eggs, frostings, dips, and even milk itself. While this is a good enrichment idea, do not get carried away with it as your body will require extra liquids to make proper use of it. (It sort of reconstitutes internally.)

Apple Juice

Apple juice is a favorite that is available year round. You can buy it bottled, as frozen concentrate or boxed concentrate. It is available with no sugar added, and of course in the fall you can often find inexpensive jugs of it. Though it is often a favorite, don't use it to the exclusion of other snack drinks.

Cranberry Drinks

The Ocean Spray people, or rather co-op, that developed the cranberry market has found wonderous and nutritious ways to combine it with other juices and in various types of packages.

Grape Juice

Bottled, this is a delicious, sugar-free drink (albeit expensive) which children enjoy. It can be stretched by adding water, lemon juice, and if necessary, some additional sweetener to it. The frozen variety does have sugar added but sugar is not the first ingredient on the label. Grape juice comes in a white variety which is nutritious and doesn't stain like its darker relative.

Fruit Nectars

Nectars are rich drinks, thicker than juices because they contain the fruit pulp. They can also be easily thinned with water or carbonated sodas. Most grocery-variety nectars contain added sugar.

Or make your own:

Apricot Nectar

½ cup dried apricots soaked in 2 cups of pineapple juice.

Whir in blender till smooth.

Tomato Juice

Tomato juice and most other vegetable juices have the advantage of being low in calories and high in nutrients. The only problem seems to be that they are also universally low in acceptance by children.

Going for the Fizz

Healthy carbonated drinks have surfaced which is great for those who find that fizz is an important part of satisfying thirst. They come with part fruit juice or just a hint of a flavor and many are sodium-free.

Do-It-Yourself Soda Pop

You can make your own pop by adding your own juice to carbonated drinks.

Fruit Fizz

Combine carbonated water with fruit juice or nectar in equal amounts. For a lighter drink, add more soda; for a heavier drink, add more juice; for a sweeter drink, add honey.

Variation: Pour the juices or syrup from canned fruit into ice cube trays and freeze. Use these cubes for flavor when serving seltzer or other plain carbonated drinks.

Paradise Punch

1 cup low calorie tropical fruit flavored drink
1 banana
2 Tbsp. powdered milk

Blend and serve.

Strawberry Slush

2 cups strawberries
¼ cup sugar

2 Tbsp. lemon juice
1 can of 7-Up (diet or regular)

Mix in blender. Add ice cubes.

Orange Froth

(This is a good afternoon drink that will serve the whole block!)

3 cups water
1 (6 oz.) can frozen orange
    juice concentrate, thawed

1 cup powdered dry milk
nutmeg, coconut powder, raw
    egg or banana (optional)

Whip ingredients together in a blender and serve.

Frozen Fruit Slush

1 can of fruit, frozen

Defrost slightly by holding can under hot running tap water for a minute or two. Open can and put contents into your blender. If the can is large, use only one or two cups of the frozen fruit. Blend to slush consistency and serve in a glass with a straw.

Hint: Try to use fruits packed in light or natural syrup to avoid unnecessary sugar.

Fruit Slurp

1 cup milk, ice milk, ice cream
    or plain yogurt
1 banana

1 peach or nectarine
a handful of strawberries

Actually you can use a combination of fresh fruits. Sweeten with honey, whip in a blender and then drink. If too thick, add ½ cup milk. This makes an excellent bedtime snack.

Banana Smoothy

1½ cups milk
1 large banana

1 Tbsp. honey
¼ tsp. vanilla

Combine in a blender and mix well. You can also use a frozen banana. (Freezing is a good way to use up extra or left-over bananas.)

Frozen Yogurt Shake

1 cup plain yogurt
1 cup ice cream or frozen
   yogurt
½ cup milk

½ cup fruit plus 1 Tbsp. jam
   (such as strawberries and
   strawberry jam)

Whir in a blender and enjoy.

Variation: A larger amount of fruit or frozen fruit would eliminate need for jam.

The Caffeine Count

Caffeine is a stimulant that affects the nervous system as well as the basic endocrine system which provides for growth and metabolism. It is a prevalent part of the adult world of drinks. Soft drinks contains a goodly amount of caffeine. Chocolate, given the quantities we sometimes eat it in, does also. We don't serve our children coffee or tea because of our concern over caffeine, yet somehow soda pops and chocolate treats are acceptable.

	Milligrams of caffeine
regular coffee (5 oz.)	100-150
instant coffee (5 oz.)	40-108
decaffeinated coffee, brewed (5 oz.)	2-5
tea, brewed (5 oz.)	20-50
ice tea in 12 oz. can	22-36
1 oz. chocolate bar	6
cocoa beverage (6 oz.)	10
Coca-Cola(12 oz.)	33
Tab (12 oz.)	32
Dr. Pepper (12 oz.)	38
Mountain Dew (12 oz.)	54

Source: Newsweek, July 19, 1982.

Chocolate and Carob

Chocolate contains caffeine and other stimulants. Some studies indicate that chocolate may aggravate migraine headaches in certain people.

Chocolate as we know it is a bitter substance when eaten by itself but is made more palatable by the addition of a lot of sugar. Cocoa powdered drink is chocolate plus sugar. Chocolate has a very high fat content—52%, in fact. Chocolate appeals to your "fat" tooth because it is the fat combined with the sugar, that makes chocolate taste so good.

Hint: Make a healthier equivalent of a 1-ounce square of chocolate by blending 3 Tbsp. cocoa with 1 Tbsp. of margarine or polyunsaturated oil.

Is there another solution to the chocolate problem? Probably. It is called carob powder and it is a substance with a taste very similar to chocolate. I resisted trying carob for a long time—another one of those "health foods"—even though I knew its fat content was low (2 percent), it had no caffeine (what child needs extra stimulation), and that it was high in natural sugars and low in starch.

There is carob powder and carob drink. In the latter, carob is combined with brown sugar to enhance its taste. When I finally tried carob I started with the drink. I did not mention it to my children, I simply gave it to them as I would a glass of chocolate milk with their lunch while they watched Sesame Street (naturally!). To my surprise, they never said a word to me about the taste or suggested that it tasted different. Depending on where or how it's used, carob can have a slightly raw taste or aftertaste. Some people recommend adding a pinch of instant coffee or using carob in vegetable oil base recipes to avoid this. Mixing one-half carob and one-half cocoa is a good way to start. In a health food store or co-op, you can also find carob chips to use in baking. Carob is worth experimenting with.

One last word on behalf of the dental community: It has been shown that frequent eating causes more cavities unless you really do brush and floss after every meal and snack. This is especially true when foods are sugared or sticky. Unfortunately this edict applies to honey and raisins as well as to candy and cake. All the snacks described herein will not make the recommended lists of all dentists.

You can please some of the nutritionists, doctors and dentists some of the time—but not all of them all of the time.

55

It's Delicious..It's (more) Nutritious...It's Dessert

If I could choose one word in our vocabulary to lose, dessert would be it. Years ago when a sweet was a treat rather than an hourly occurrance, dessert was the luxurious finish to a meal. Today we can get as much sugar along with our meals (such as our breakfast cereals and soft drinks) as in dessert.

My all time favorite dessert recipe is:

"Notto Haveone"

> 0 cups flour
> 0 cups sugar
> 0 tsp. salt
> no dash of anything

Easy to make, inexpensive and nonfattening, no dishes to clean and second helpings are never a problem.

If you prefer a dessert with more taste and texture, the next consideration would be fruit, cheese and crackers, or all three. Or maybe a large bowl of unshelled nuts served with nutcrackers and toothpicks.

"But my husband would feel denied," you claim. Or, "My children would threaten to move in with the neighbors" (now there's an appealing idea!). However, if you are going to cut back on the 100 plus pounds of refined sugar consumed per person each year in your family, this is obviously the place to start.

Perhaps the enormity of all this excess sugar consumption has already hit home if you have one or more overweight children. The easiest and fastest way to achieve obesity is with excess sugar. Early fat can determine the number of fat cells we carry into adulthood, making obesity an almost inescapable problem. While the best remedy for excess weight is regular exercise, the second best is to cut back on refined sugar consumption and the third best is to cut back on refined flour consumption.

Less (sugar) is better, so here are some ideas to help make a dent in your sugar consumption. A few of the recipes have more sugar than I like to use but at least these recipes have other ingredients to give them some "redeeming value." In other words, if you persist in the sweetened route, at least get something for your money...I mean, your body.

Junket

(*Pudding you can make without artificial colorings and flavorings.*)

2 cups milk
⅔ cup powdered milk
¼ cup white or brown sugar or 2 Tbsp. honey
1 tsp. vanilla
1 rennet tablet

Combine milk, powdered milk and sweetener in a saucepan. Heat until lukewarm, 110°. Temperature is very important. Meanwhile dissolve rennet tablet in 1 Tbsp. of water and stir into warm milk no longer than 10 *seconds*. Pour into custard cups. DO NOT MOVE CUPS UNTIL JUNKET IS SET, which takes about 10 minutes.

Rennet tablets, if not found next to the unflavored gelatin envelopes in your grocery store, may be found in drugstores. They are quite inexpensive.

Variation: Sweeten to taste with molasses instead of sugar or honey. Omit vanilla and flavor to taste with almond extract or freshly shredded orange rind or lemon rind. Before adding rennet tablet, stir into milk ½ cup of graham cracker crumbs or toasted wheat germ or Grape Nuts. Add a sprinkle of cinnamon.

Pudding Parfait

1 (17 oz.) can rice pudding
1 (16 oz.) can mandarin orange sections, drained, or
    fresh orange slices

Mix the chilled rice pudding with the orange sections. Spoon the mixture into a parfait glass.

Variation: Tapioca, bought or homemade, can be substituted for the rice pudding.

Banana Custard

(*This tastes like banana cream pie, but without a crust.*)

3 egg yolks	1 tsp. vanilla
1 whole egg	3 egg whites
1½ cups milk	½ tsp. cream of tartar
½ cup sugar	4 Tbsp. sugar
½ cup flour	1 large banana

In a heavy saucepan beat egg yolks and the one whole egg. Add milk and the combined sugar and flour. Stir continously over low heat until mixture thickens. Remove from heat, add vanilla and let cool. Now beat egg whites with cream of tartar till frothy. Add remaining sugar and continue beating till egg whites form stiff peaks. Pour half of the custard mixture evenly divided among six custard cups. Evenly distribute sliced banana over custard. Pour remaining custard into cups. Spoon egg white mixture over custard, sealing to edges of cups. Bake at 350° for 10 minutes, about the time it takes to brown on top.

Apple Snow Fluff

2 egg whites	cinnamon
1 cup of cold applesauce	dash of lemon juice
2 tsp. sugar or artificial sweetener	

Beat egg whites until stiff but not dry, add sugar or artificial sweetener. Add the lemon juice to the cold applesauce. Fold the stiff egg whites into the applesauce then spoon into individual cups. Top each dish with a dash of cinnamon.

Frosty Cranberry Cupcakes

1 cup sour cream
¼ cup powdered sugar

1 (16 oz.) can whole
   cranberry sauce
1 (8 oz.) can crushed
   pineapple, undrained

Combine sour cream with powdered sugar. Stir in cranberry sauce and pineapple with liquid. Pour into cupcake liners, or into 9 x 13-inch pan for bars. Freeze. Remove from freezer 10 minutes before serving.

Variation: Use frozen strawberries instead of cranberry sauce.

Frozen Yogurt

1 (8 oz.) container of plain yogurt
1 cup strawberries, blueberries or banana slices
sweeten to taste (optional)

Whip this mixture in your blender. Put blender container into freezer for ½ hour. Remove and blend again. Repeat once or twice more, then pour into bowl or popsicle molds. If you don't have a blender, use a mixer.

Variation: Canned fruit also works well, especially pineapple. Also, serve frozen yogurt—frozen or simply refrigerated till firm—in ice cream cones.

Jell-Yo

1 (6 oz.) can frozen juice
   concentrate, thawed
1 envelope unflavored gelatin
1 cup water

½ cup sugar or corn syrup
1 (8 oz.) container of plain
   yogurt

Soften gelatin in juice. In a saucepan, heat water to boiling, add gelatin/juice mixture, and sugar. Stir till dissolved. Remove from heat, cool for 5 minutes, add yogurt and mix well. Pour into bowl or individual dishes. Refrigerate till set.

Variation: Add contents of 1 small package of Jell-O™ to 1 cup water. Heat to boiling. Cool and add plain yogurt. Let set in refrigerator.

Danish Turnovers

2 oz. (½ cup) cottage cheese
⅛ tsp. cinnamon
⅛ tsp. vanilla

1 Tbsp. sugar or honey
1 pkg. refrigerated crescent
  rolls

Thoroughly combine first four ingredients. Use as filler for crescent rolls, then fold to form "Danish pastry" triangles. Bake at 375° till rolls are browned.

Variation: Spoon filling on whole wheat toast. Heat in oven or toaster oven until bubbly.

Peanut Butter Fondue

(*Fun as well as good tasting!*)

1 cup creamy peanut butter
1 cup light cream
½ cup (8 Tbsp.) honey
apple wedges
peach quarters
pear quarters

banana chunks
pitted dates
fresh whole strawberries
flaked coconut and/or toasted
  wheat germ (optional)

Place peanut butter in fondue pot. Gradually stir in cream and honey. Place over low heat, stirring constantly until mixture starts to boil. Keep warm on the table while serving. Spear fruit on fondue fork and dip into peanut butter mixture. Coat with coconut and/or toasted wheat germ if you wish.

Super Fridge Fudge

½ cup (8 Tbsp.) honey
½ cup (8 Tbsp.) peanut butter
½ cup cocoa powder or carob
½ cup raisins or dates
½-1 cup shredded coconut

2 cups total, any combination
  of sesame seeds,
  sunflower seeds and
  chopped nuts

Heat honey and peanut butter. Quickly add cocoa powder or carob and stir. Remove from heat. Add seeds, nuts, coconut and dried fruit. Pour into a square, greased pan and refrigerate to harden. Cut in squares. Keep stored in refrigerator.

Better-For-You-Brownies

¼ cup oil
1 Tbsp. molasses
1 cup brown sugar
2 tsp. vanilla
2 eggs
½ cup broken pecans or
    walnuts

1 cup wheat germ
⅔ cup powdered milk
½ tsp. baking powder
¼ cup cocoa powder or carob
    or 2 sq. unsweetened
    baking chocolate

Mix together all ingredients except dry milk, baking powder and cocoa or carob powder. If using squares of chocolate, melt in a double boiler and add at this point. Combine dry milk, baking powder and carob. Stir into wet ingredients. Spread in a heavily greased 8 x 8-inch pan and bake at 350° for approximately 30 minutes. Turn out of pan and cut into bars while still warm.

Hint: Sprinkle with powdered sugar.

Carob Brownie Bars

½ cup butter or margarine,
    softened
¾ cup honey
2 eggs
1 tsp. vanilla

½ cup whole wheat pastry
    flour
3 Tbsp. carob powder
½ cup walnuts, chopped

Preheat oven to 350° and grease an 8-inch square pan. In a medium-size mixing bowl, beat together the butter or margarine and honey until creamy. Add eggs and vanilla and beat to combine. In another bowl stir together the flour and carob. Add to the other mixture and beat a minute or so. Then stir in walnuts and pour into pan. Bake 20 to 30 minutes, but watch carefully so that it doesn't overcook. Remove from oven, cool, and cut into bars. Serve topped with vanilla ice cream.

Apple Pie Bread Bars

3 eggs
1 (20 oz.) can of Apple Pie
    Filling

2 (7 oz.) envelopes of Apple
    Spice Muffin Mix

Beat eggs. Add pie filling and dry mix till blended. Bake 350° for 40 minutes in a 8 x 8-inch pan; or for 1½ hours in a loaf pan.

Cranberry Squares

1 cup (2 sticks) butter or
  margarine
1 cup brown sugar
1 cup flour (white or half white,
  half whole wheat)
2½ cups oatmeal, uncooked

1 (16 oz.) can whole
  cranberry sauce or 2
  cups of homemade
  cranberry sauce
½ cup toasted wheat germ
  (optional)

Mix butter, brown sugar, flour, oatmeal (and wheat germ) together. Work with fingers until mixture is in crumbs the size of peas. Pat half the mixture into an 8-inch pan. Spread cranberry sauce over it and top with remainder of mixture. Pat down gently. Bake at 375° for 30 minutes or till lightly browned. Cut into squares while still warm.

Cheese Cake Bars

(Fattening but delicious! How I envy those kids with all that energy to burn fat that doesn't go to their hips as it does to mine.)

1 cup flour (white or half white,
  half whole wheat)
⅓ cup brown sugar, packed
6 Tbsp. butter or margarine,
  softened
1 (8 oz.) pkg. cream cheese,
  softened
¼ cup sugar

1 egg
2 Tbsp. milk
2 Tbsp. lemon juice
½ tsp. vanilla
2 Tbsp. chopped walnuts
2 Tbsp. toasted wheat germ
2 Tbsp. oatmeal, uncooked

In a large mixing bowl combine flour and brown sugar. Cut in butter till mixture forms fine crumbs. Reserve 1 cup crumbs for topping. Press remainder into bottom of an ungreased 8-inch square pan. Bake in oven at 350° for 15 minutes or till lightly browned. With a mixer, cream together cream cheese and sugar. Then add egg, milk, lemon juice and vanilla. Beat well. Spread batter on baked crust. Combine walnuts, crumb mixture, wheat germ and oatmeal and sprinkle over all. Bake at 350° for 20-25 minutes. Cool and cut into squares.

desserts

Easy Apple Crisp

4-6 apples, peeled, cored and
  sliced
1 Tbsp. lemon juice
1 cup oatmeal, uncooked
⅓ cup flour (white or whole
  wheat)

⅓ cup packed brown sugar
1 tsp. cinnamon
⅓ cup melted butter or
  margarine
¼ cup toasted wheat germ
  (optional)

Place apple slices in a greased 9-inch baking pan. Sprinkle with lemon juice. Combine dry ingredients and mix in melted butter until mixture is crumbly. Sprinkle over apples. Bake at 375° until apples are tender (20-30 minutes). Serve warm or cold.

Hint: Top with milk, cream or ice cream.

Hint: In the fall when apples are in season and you can't face another jar of applesauce, buy some small aluminum pans and cook up several Easy Apple Crisps to put in the freezer.

Peach Crumble

1 (29 oz.) can sliced cling
  peaches, drained
2 Tbsp. lemon juice
¼ tsp. cinnamon
1 Tbsp. butter or margarine
¼ cup melted shortening
⅓ cup brown sugar

⅓ cup flour (white or half
  white, half whole wheat)
¼ tsp. baking soda
⅔ cup oatmeal, uncooked
½ tsp. vanilla
ice cream or cream or milk
  (optional)

Arrange peaches in buttered shallow 1 quart baking dish. Sprinkle with lemon juice and cinnamon. Dot with butter. Combine shortening and sugar in a bowl. Add rest of ingredients. Crumble with fingers and sprinkle on peaches. Bake at 350° for 45 minutes. Makes four servings. Top with ice cream or cream or milk when ready to serve.

Hint: Peaches canned in light syrup or own juice would be preferable.

Date Bars

1-¼ cup pitted dates
⅓ cup sugar
½ cup water

Combine these ingredients in a saucepan and cook over medium heat. Stir to mash the dates. When uniformly soft, remove from heat and cool.

¾ cup butter or margarine
¾ cup brown sugar
1 cup flour (white or whole wheat)

2 cups oatmeal
1 tsp. baking soda

Blend these five ingredients well and grease half of the mixture into the bottom of a greased and floured 8 to 9-inch square pan. Spread date mixture over the pressed crumb mixture. Top with remainder of the dry ingredients. Bake at 350° for 45 minutes or till the top is browned.

Raisin-Nut Bars

½ cup (1 stick) butter or margarine, melted
⅓ cup sugar
⅓ cup packed brown sugar
¼ cup applesauce
1 egg
1 tsp. vanilla

1 cup flour (whole wheat or white)
1 tsp. baking powder
½ tsp. cinnamon
½ cup (or more) raisins
½ cup (or more) chopped nuts

Combine melted butter or margarine with sugars, applesauce, egg and vanilla. Combine flour, baking powder and cinnamon. Blend wet and dry mixtures then add raisins and nuts. Bake in a greased 9-inch square pan for 30 minutes at 350°. Let cool before cutting into bars.

Cottage Cheese Cookies

1 cup (2 sticks) butter or margarine, softened
1 cup creamed cottage cheese, small curd
2 cups flour (white or half white, half whole wheat)
strawberry preserves or any other filling

Cream together butter and cottage cheese. Work in flour and wrap dough in waxed paper. Place in refrigerator to harden. When cold, roll in thin sheets and cut into 3-inch squares and place on a lightly greased cookie sheet. Place a teaspoon of preserves (or honey) in center of each square and fold into a triangle, pressing edges together very firmly. Bake in preheated 350° oven for 15 minutes or until crust is brown and crisp.

Colossal Cookies!

These recipes can be used to make ordinary-sized cookies, or to make the oversized 'Colossal' cookies which kids adore! Directions for Colossal Cookies follow the third recipe.

Crunchy Chocolatey Cookies

1 cup flour (white or half white, half whole wheat)
3 Tbsp. cocoa or carob
¼ tsp. baking soda
¼ tsp. baking powder
½ cup sugar or ¾ cup honey
½ cup (1 stick) butter or margarine
1 egg
1 tsp. vanilla

Combine flour, cocoa (or carob), baking soda and baking powder and mix well. Then combine softened butter or margarine, sweetener, vanilla and egg. Combine wet and dry ingredients together and mix well.

For Colossal Cookies, use ⅓ cup of dough per cookie. Makes 4-6 cookies.

Oatmeal-Raisin Cookies

1 cup (2 sticks) butter or margarine
1½ cups brown sugar
2 cups flour (white, whole wheat or half and half)
2 eggs, beaten
1 tsp. vanilla
2⅓ cups oatmeal, uncooked
2 tsp. baking soda
1 tsp. cinnamon
1½ cups raisins

Cream butter, sugar and then add eggs and vanilla. Separately combine dry ingredients then mix well with creamed mixture. Add raisins.

For Colossal Cookies, use ½ cup of dough per cookie. Makes 10-12 cookies.

Chocolate Chip Cookies

The unbeatable best of the chocolate cookie recipes is the Original Toll House Cookie recipe found on the back of Nestle's semi-sweet chocolate morsels bag. It can be altered slightly—without loss of taste—by not using the salt called for and by using the Cornell Triple Rich Formula (see page 124). And, of course there is no need to use the *whole* 12 oz. bag of chocolate morsels.

For Colossal Cookies, use ½ cup of dough per cookie. Makes 8-10 terrific cookies.

To make Colossal Cookies:

Spoon dough onto a greased cookie sheet. Start out with not more than two at a time till you judge how much they spread and how big you want them. Lightly grease the bottom of pie pan. Dip it into flour or sugar and use it to flatten each cookie into a 5 to 6-inch circle. Make sure each cookie is a least 2 inches from the edge. Baking time is 12-15 minutes at 350°.

To seal each cookie in plastic wrap:

Wrap each cookie in a piece of clear plastic sufficient to completely cover cookie. Put a piece of brown heavy paper on a cookie sheet. Place wrapped cookies (as many as fit without overlapping) on the brown paper and put in 325° oven for 30 seconds until plastic shrinks tightly over the cookie. Remove and cool. Store sealed for a week or freeze for longer storage.

Cookie Clusters

2 squares white bark
½ cup (8 Tbsp.) peanut butter

4 cups granola
4 cups chow mein noodles

Melt the 2 squares of white bark in a 200° oven for 20 minutes in a 12 x 9 x 2-inch pan. Remove from the oven when completely softened and add peanut butter and mix well. In a bowl combine granola and noodles. Add this mixture to melted bark and peanut butter. Toss and coat mixture evenly. Drop by the tablespoon onto aluminum foil or wax paper. These cookies harden upon cooling completely. Makes 4 dozen.

Hint: Food co-ops often have delicious whole wheat chow mein noodles.

Whipped Cream Graham Cake

(*A good make-ahead treat!*)

1 pint (2 cups) heavy cream
2 Tbsp. honey or sugar
32 squares (16 rectangles) of
    graham crackers
sprinkles

Beat cream with sweetener until stiff. Spread whipped cream heavily on one square and place it on a platter. Spread cream heavily on a second square and place it on top of the first. Continue until there is a stack of 4 squares. Press down gently on the top square so the cream squeezes out of the sides. Spread the excess along the sides. Repeat this procedure until there are eight stacks. Slide them together till sides touch to form a rectangular cake of 2 squares by 4 squares. Use extra whipped cream to smooth over all the tops. Refrigerate. Allowing it to chill several hours before serving enables the crackers to soften. A dash of sprinkles over the top adds a party flavor without adding much additional sugar. Serves 8.

Hint: Use a pressurized can of whipped cream if you don't have the time or inclination to whip the cream.

Unbirthday Cake

(*A chocolatey treat which will make any day special. Moist— heavy— delicious!*

4 eggs, separated
1 cup sugar
½ cup (8 Tbsp.) honey
1 cup whole wheat flour
1½ cups white flour

4 Tbsp. cocoa powder or
    carob
2 tsp. baking powder
2 cups sour cream
1 tsp. vanilla

Beat egg whites till frothy, add yolks and beat again. Add sweeteners and whole wheat flour. Mix well. Add cocoa and baking soda to white flour and stir into mixture alternately with sour cream. Stir in vanilla. Bake in a greased, floured bundt pan at 350° for 50 minutes. Equally delectable baked in two greased and floured 9-inch pans or a large rectangular pan (30 minutes) or in 24 cupcake holders (20 minutes).

Angel's Delight

A wonderful party or any day dessert is angel food cake (store bought) topped with frozen whipped topping and fresh strawberries. It's less than 200 calories per serving.

Carrot Cake

(or *Uncle Wiggly's Delight!*)

1 cup oil
2½ cups grated carrots
    (approx. 3 large carrots)
1-¼ cups brown sugar
¼ cup honey

4 eggs, beaten
2 tsp. baking soda
2 cups flour (white or half
    white, half whole wheat)
2 tsp. cinnamon

Combine first five ingredients and mix well. Add combined soda, flour and cinnamon. Bake in a greased and floured 13 x 9-inch pan at 325° for 40-45 minutes. Cream cheese frosting (page 73) is the topping recommended here.

Hint: Defrost a 20 oz. bag of frozen cut carrots. Chop one cup at a time in a blender. Use whole amount as called for in above recipe.

Zucchini Bread

(*It tastes a whole lot better than it sounds!*)

2½ cups flour (white or half
    white, half whole wheat)
¼ cup powdered milk
½ cup wheat germ
2 tsp. baking soda
½ tsp. baking powder
2 cups sugar (1 brown, 1
    white)

3 tsp. cinnamon
½ tsp. nutmeg
1 cup oil
3 eggs, beaten
3 tsp. vanilla
1 cup chopped nuts
2 cups (3 medium size)
    zucchini, with peel, grated

Combine above ingredients and bake in a well greased loaf pan at 350° for one hour. This recipe makes two loaves.

Hint: To grate zucchini quickly, place zucchini cut into chunks in a blender. Cover with water and blend at "chop" for a few seconds till processed. Drain off water and use.

Little-Bit-Of-Chocolate Bars

(A small amount of chocolate goes a long way to help down these delicious—albeit slightly dry—*bars.)*

½ cup (1 stick) butter or margarine
½ cup brown sugar, packed
1 tsp. vanilla
1 egg

1½ cups flour (white or half white, half whole wheat)
1 cup regular wheat germ
½ cup semi-sweet chocolate chips

Cream butter and brown sugar in a large bowl. Beat in vanilla and egg. Stir in flour and wheat germ. Press evenly into an 8-inch square baking pan. Bake at 325° for 20 minutes or till lightly browned. Remove from oven and immediately sprinkle top with chocolate chips. When the chocolate has softened, use a spatula or broad knife to spread it carefully over the top surface. Cool before cutting into bars. To store, separate layers with foil.

Applesauce Cake

⅔ cups margarine, melted
1 cup sugar (less than 1 cup if using sweetened applesauce)
2 cups flour (white or half white, and half whole wheat)

1½ cups unsweetened applesauce-*hot*
2 tsp. baking soda
1 heaping tsp. cinnamon
1 cup raisins
1 cup nuts (optional)
2 Tbsp. wheat germ (optional)

Pour melted shortening into *hot* applesauce. Add sugar. Sift in flour, baking soda and cinnamon. Add raisins, nuts and wheat germ. Bake in a greased 9 x 13-inch pan at 375° for 1 hour or in two 8-inch pans for 25 minutes and have one to freeze. Good while still warm topped with powdered sugar or whipped cream.

Hint: When cutting cake, let one child cut and the other have the first choice. You'll be delighted at how fairly this works.

Banana Bread

¼ cup butter or margarine
½ cup brown sugar
1 egg, beaten
1 cup bran cereal or
  uncooked oatmeal
4-5 mashed ripe bananas
  (about 1½ cups)

1 tsp. vanilla
1½ cups flour (white, whole
  wheat or a combination)
2 tsp. baking powder
½ tsp. baking soda
½ cup chopped nuts

Cream shortening and sugar until light. Add egg and mix. Then add the cereal, bananas and vanilla. Stir. Combine the remaining ingredients in a bowl and add to the first mixture, stirring only long enough to moisten the flour. Bake in a greased loaf pan at 350° for an hour or until bread tests as done.

Wholesome Poundcake

1 cup (2 sticks) butter or
  margarine
2 cups packed brown sugar
2 tsp. flavoring, vanilla or
  almond
3 eggs
¼ cup raw wheat germ

2 cups flour (white, whole
  wheat or half and half)
½ tsp. baking soda
1 cup plain yogurt
½ cup nuts or granola
  (optional)

With an electric mixer, beat together butter and brown sugar. Add in flavorings and eggs and beat till smooth. Combine flour, wheat germ and soda in a bowl and mix. Add flour mixture alternately with yogurt to batter, blending well after each addition. Bake at 325° in two greased and floured loaf pans or one tube pan for about one hour. Cool for ½ hour before removing from the pans.

Hint: The unused balance of cookie and cake desserts can be stored in the freezer. Cakes are best sliced and wrapped individually for freezing. This method reduces the possibility that one member of the family will polish off any left out leftovers.

Frostings

It's not hard to make your own frostings. They are so superior in taste and quality to any form of commercial mix that once you have found one or two favorites you won't want to settle for second best. Good-for-you frostings work fine on muffins and breads as well as on cookies and cakes.

Whipped Cream

Whipped cream contains no chemicals and can be prepared from scratch very quickly. You can flavor it yourself.

1 pint heavy or whipping cream
2 tsp. honey or sugar

In a bowl combine cream and sweetener. Whip with an electric mixer or egg beater until mix is fluffy and holds its shape.

Variation: Whip cream nearly stiff. Add ½ cup powdered milk and whip 30 seconds. Dissolve 1 envelope of unflavored gelatin in 1 Tbsp. of cold water, then heat till clear. Add to the half whipped cream and finish whipping. Cream will hold its shape nicely.

Non-Fat Whipped Topping

½ cup instant non-fat dry milk   1 tsp. vanilla (optional)
¼ cup ice cold water   ½ tsp. almond extract (optional)
1 Tbsp. lemon juice

Use a chilled metal bowl and beaters. Beat milk and water for 2-3 minutes until soft peaks form. Add lemon juice (and/or vanilla and almond extract). Beat again for 1-2 minutes. Chill. This will hold for ½ hour and makes about 1½ cups topping.

You've-Got-Chocolate-On-My-Peanut-Butter Frosting

½ cup (8 Tbsp.) peanut butter
1 (6 oz.) pkg. chocolate chips

Melt peanut butter and chocolate chips together over medium heat until smooth and spreadable.

Cream Cheese Frosting

3 oz. cream cheese
⅓ cup butter or margarine,
    softened
1 tsp. vanilla

1½ cups powdered sugar
toasted wheat germ or
    chopped nuts (optional)

Whip together cream cheese and butter. Add vanilla and powdered sugar. If too stiff for spreading, thin with a little milk. Sprinkle with a nutty topping, if desired.

Variation: 8 oz. cream cheese, 2 Tbsp. honey, and a ¼ cup heavy cream should be whipped till fluffy. Combine cream cheese and honey. Mix with whipped cream.

Brown Sugar Frosting

Blend together:

3 Tbsp. butter or margarine,
    softened
½ cup canned evaporated
    milk

1 tsp. maple or vanilla
    flavorings
½ cup or more of powdered milk
1½ cups brown sugar

Peanut Butter Frosting

Combine:

1 cup powdered sugar
¼ cup cream cheese
¼ cup powdered milk

½ cup peanut butter
¼ cup milk

Mix till smooth and then spread.

Nutty Topping

½ cup maple syrup
4 oz. walnuts, pecans, or cashews

Pulverize nuts in a blender. Mix with syrup to a paste. Spread!

If you are still using the powdered sugar-plus-a-bit-of water combination for an icing, keep in mind that the liquid used can also be orange juice, lemon juice, or yogurt.

To Decorate

- Any frosting can be squeezed from a small plastic bag with one corner cut out.

- For natural frosting or icing colorings, add a bit of cranberry juice for pink; carrot juice for yellow/orange; grape juice concentrate for a dark pink; crushed blueberries for blue, etc.

- Melt a handful of chocolate chips to use as "paint" to inscribe names and greetings with a clean watercolor brush on birthday cakes, cookies, even sandwiches.

- You can also paint melted chocolate on wax paper to be removed when it hardens; and use this technique to make your own chocolate money by painting on clean, greased coins. Apply thickly!

Ice Cream

I've delayed talking about ice cream as long as I could because I really have mixed emotions about it. Basically my family and I LOVE IT. We love it expensive, cheap, at the local franchise or homemade on the Fourth of July. Our taste buds have a wide range of acceptance...gluttony might be a more apt description.

Good ice cream, I discovered when I began to make my own, is fattening because of the large amount of cream, not sugar, that is used. Commercial manufacturers can more readily afford sugar than real cream, and artificial flavorings than fruits.

I have finally opted for the better, more expensive ice creams and I dispense them more frugally. Ice cream, frozen yogurts and soft serve ice cream are tasty ways to get the food value of milk products.

Hint: Storing ice cream containers in a plastic bag before putting them in the freezer will help prevent ice crystals from forming.

Making your own is simplified by current offerings in your kitchenware center. A major disadvantage of homemade ice cream is that it is apt to freeze too hard. It does not contain chemical emulsifiers to keep it fluffy, and raising your freezer's temperature to soften ice cream would adversely affect other foods in the freezer. However, if you are making your own, here is my favorite recipe which can be flavored to please your particular taste:

Basic Vanilla Ice Cream

2 cups heavy cream
2 eggs separated
½ cup sugar or honey

1 tsp. vanilla
dash of salt

Whip two cups of heavy cream in a blender till fairly thick. Add egg yolks, sweetener, vanilla and salt. Blend to mix. Beat egg whites stiff. Combine with cream mixture.

If you are just using your blender, place blender container holding the mixture into your freezer for ½ hour. Take out and blend 1 minute. Repeat this one or two times more, then pour into freezing container. If it doesn't beat efficiently in your blender you will need to use a mixing bowl and an electric beater.

Do-It-Yourself Sundaes

When serving ice cream, offer some of the following toppings:

- **Nuts**—peanuts, walnuts, cashews, sliced almonds

- **Sauces**—honey, maple syrup, chocolate syrup in small amounts

- **Fruits**—chopped dates, apricots, berries, banana slices, pineapple, cherries, sliced peaches

- **And Other Goodies**—carob or chocolate chips, granola, shredded coconut, toasted wheat germ, whipped cream or a non-dairy whipped topping

Carob Fudge Sauce

(*To top off any sundae!*)

⅓ cup carob powder
1 tsp. cornstarch
1 small (5.3 oz.) can
   evaporated milk

⅓ cup honey
¼ cup butter
1 tsp. vanilla

Stir together the carob powder, cornstarch and evaporated milk until there are no lumps. Do this in a blender. Pour the mixture into a medium- size saucepan. Add honey and cook, stirring constantly over medium heat until mixture thickens and boils. Remove from heat and stir in butter and vanilla. Makes ¾ cup.

Other frozen figures:

- The term "French" ice cream means that a good percentage of egg solids has been added which is why it usually looks more yellow.

- The average scoop of ice cream contains 135 calories versus a Dove Bar that has 497 calories. If you want to watch those calories, try vanilla ice milk which contains one-third the calories of the gourmet ice creams. Ice milk has lower fat content because it contains less milk fats than ice cream.

- Sherbet is chemically similar in composition to ice cream but it has a still lower milk content and extra sugar is added to offset a high acid content.

- Only water ices contain no milk.

Very Berry Ices

1 pt. fresh berries
¾ cup sugar or honey

¾ cup water
¼ cup orange or lemon juice

Puree fruit in a blender. Heat water and sweetener together to a clear syrup and pour into blender. Mix completely. Freeze in plastic containers or as popsicles.

The variety of water-based frozen novelties in the grocery store offers treats for every pocket book. As in most cases, you are going to get what you pay for. Do check out the labels. The number of available items as juice bars should satisfy your child's palate.

I must confess to feeling ambivalent about using dessert as a reward. I understand that this practice may lead to obesity or overeating problems later in life. I do try to prepare foods that will appeal to my children, and I try not to become (too) upset if they don't eat everything. But if, for any reason, they do not finish the better part of their meals, I don't think they should expect to be served dessert. Needless to say, the possibility of "no dessert" is responsible for the consumption of a good deal more fish, soups, salads and vegetables than would otherwise be the case.

If Your Child Can't Drink Milk

It's surprising how little practical information is available to parents of children who can't drink milk. Milk intolerance is a common problem that defies the slogan "MILK IS FOR EVERYBODY." It is not. Actually, the majority of the world's population cannot tolerate cow's milk. Most able are those of Western European descent and even among this group a significant percentage (20%) can't tolerate milk. Symptoms such as abdominal pain, bloating, gas, diarrhea, or nausea may well be related to the ingestion of cow's milk. This intolerance is due to an inability to digest the natural sugar in milk and is referred to as lactose intolerance. An enzyme in the intestinal lining named "lactase," breaks down lactose (milk sugar) into simple digestible sugars. When lactase is completely absent (a rare condition) or present in low concentrations (more common), consumption of milk products may cause discomfort. In a young child, an intestinal infection can cause a temporary reduction of lactase. (This is one reason why doctors eliminate milk when a child has diarrhea.)

The amount of milk tolerable to those with lactose intolerance varies with the level of lactase in the intestine. For example, some persons who cannot digest moderate amounts of milk can tolerate natural yogurt or aged cheeses.

It is generally believed that mother's milk never causes digestive problems for a new baby. However, if a baby has a complete lactase deficiency (which is very rare), he or she will not be able to tolerate even breast milk. Fortunately today, soy-based formulas are available for babies having trouble digesting milk for whatever reason. Infant soy formula is balanced to provide good growth. Feeding soy formula to an infant is an uncomplicated task because, like other ready-to-feed formulas, it is available in liquid form. Soy formula or soy milk powder is made from soy beans, a good source of protein and calcium which is easy to digest.

Foods to Avoid

When solid foods replace formula and food choices broaden, selection becomes challenging. If all milk is restricted, it will be necessary to read labels on every package of processed food before buying. Even then, the FDA doesn't require the listing of all consumable products, and lactose, a popular food and drug filler, may not be listed.

Here is a list of foods which contain milk or milk-sugar by-products. Some are obvious inclusions, others are surprising:

Milk and Milk Products

Milk (cream, sour cream, cream cheese, skim,
      evaporated, condensed, butter, cheese, buttermilk,
      powdered, yogurt, most margarines)
Imitation sour cream
Ice cream, ice milk, sherbet
Cream soups and chowders
Vegetables frozen in butter or cheese sauces

Sugar Products

Frostings
Buttered syrups
Milk chocolate
Candy containing milk or milk chocolate
Caramels, toffees
Some chewing gums
Cookies, boxed and bakery
Many sugar substitutes (Sweet and Low)
Molasses

Bread and Grain Products

Most breads (important to check labels)
Many crackers
Popovers
Croutons

Other

Prepared mixes for baked goods
Canned spaghetti and other pastas
Most hot dogs, bolognas, liverwurst and other cold cuts
Canned meats, spreads
Foods fried in batter
Frozen fish sticks
Pressed chicken rolls
Frozen egg substitutes
Many dry cereals
Salad dressing when cheese has been added
Gravies
Vitamin capsules and medications using lactose fillers

The words on labels to watch for are: milk (condensed, evaporated, fresh, whole, skim), buttermilk, sweet or sour cream, malted milk, lactose, non-fat dry milk solids, curds, whey, margarine, butter, sodium caseinate, casein and lactalbumin. (The last three are additives made from the protein of cow's milk and are permissible for those who cannot tolerate lactose—milk sugar—but not for those who are allergic to milk.)

Again, keep in mind that milk intolerance is often a matter of degree. Some children tolerate more milk products than others. Fortunately some children outgrow this but for others it is a question of adjusting milk and milk-product intake to a comfortable level. A complete lactose intolerance present at birth will not be outgrown, however.

It is essential to consult with a pediatrician before removing milk from a child's diet. Do not make a diagnosis yourself!

Discuss your child's diet with your pediatrician to be sure that enough protein and calcium, the main nutritional benefits of milk, are being provided from your limited food selection. Other protein rich foods are meat, poultry, tofu, eggs, dried beans, nuts, peanut butter, fish, pork and lamb. Milk and milk-products are our most important source of calcium. Although minimal compared with milk, other calcium rich foods are sardines, soybeans, dried figs, cauliflower, broccoli, green olives, spinach, dates, dried apricots, raisins, dried prunes, limes, scallions, and green beans.

In order to get roughly the equivalent of calcium contained in 1 quart of milk, one would have to eat any of the following foods:

3 loaves of bread   4 lbs. of dates
2 lbs. of dried figs   9-10 lbs. of green beans
4 lbs. of broccoli

If your child's diet is completely milk-free your pediatrician, no doubt, will add a calcium supplement. Calcium supports bone growth which is crucial during fast growth years.

There is one product available which does make milk digestible for the lactose-intolerant person. It is called LactAid and comes as a bottle of lactase enzyme which can be added to a quart of milk. It will break down 75 percent of the lactose present. In some parts of the country fresh milk treated with LactAid is available in grocery stores. For a free starter kit containing 6 tablets, call 1-800-LACTAID. Or write for information to Consumer Services, Lactaid, Inc., P.O. Box 1100, Pleasantville, NJ 08232.

Check your health food store for other products, such as Milk Gest, which aid in milk digestion. These products are tablets of lactase plus rennin which must be taken before or during a meal (afterwards is too late).

A lactose intolerance is only one of several reasons your child might be taken off milk. Some children are simply "allergic" (sneezing and wheezing) to milk. Regardless of the origins of your problem, here are some cooking ideas to make life a bit more tolerable.

Cooking Milk-Free

In cooking you can very often substitute another liquid for the quantity of milk called for. Soy powdered milk can be reconstituted and is available in health food stores, supermarkets or drug stores. Some non-dairy coffee lighteners are useful but be sure the one you select omits lactose. Infant soy formula may be palatable in some recipes or used on cereals. When a recipe calls for milk or cream, try water, chicken stock, beef stock, wine or fruit juices. Orange juice and apple juice—even 7-Up®—work nicely in many recipes for baked products. With a bit of experimenting you'll find substitutes of your own that work.

Meal Ideas

Milk-Free Breakfasts

Use margarines that don't contain milk or milk products found in your grocery's refrigerated dairy case or freezer section.

French Toast

1 egg	a drop of vanilla
½ tsp. water or orange juice	1 slice milk-free bread
dash of cinnamon	1 Tbsp. milk-free margarine

Beat egg in a shallow bowl with water or juice, cinnamon and vanilla. Soak bread in liquid till all is absorbed. Melt milk-free margarine or shortening in a pan. Brown soaked toast on one side, flip and brown on the other. Serve with syrup (no butter) or jam, or make a sandwich by using a slice of ham or bacon between slices of French toast.

Pancakes

Make your own batter. Most prepared mixes contain dry milk solids. Instead of milk, substitute coffee lightener, soy milk or orange juice mixed with water. Add corn oil, vegetable shortening or milk-free margarine. You'll hardly notice the difference from pancakes made with milk.

Banana Bread

¾ cup vegetable shortening
½ cup brown sugar
½ cup white sugar
2 eggs
½ tsp. vanilla or orange
   extract

dash of salt
1 cup very ripe bananas,
   mashed
1 cup whole wheat flour
¾ cup white flour
4 tsp. baking powder

Cream shortening and sugar. Beat in eggs and extract. Add mashed bananas. Sift in flour, baking powder and salt. Mix thoroughly. Bake in a greased loaf pan at 350° for 55 minutes.

Muffins

Follow your usual recipe or any given on boxes of milk-free cereal but use the liquid of your choice instead of milk.

Of course there are always hot cereals (not instant Cream of Wheat; read labels carefully) and soft or hard-cooked eggs. You also need to read dry cereal labels carefully because so many, including most granola types, contain milk. Milk substitutes, even orange juice, taste pretty good over dry cereal. Keep in mind that most egg substitutes contain milk.

Milk-Free Lunches

Peanut butter is a good protein source, fine on milk-free bread or toast. Also meats, egg salad, soups (not cream ones), milk-free hot dogs (the kosher kind), milk-free cold cuts, mild chili con carne, spaghetti with meat sauce (use any leftover meat), tacos (the shells should be milk-free) with meat, shredded lettuce or spinach.

Tunaburgers

1 can tuna, drained
1 egg
½ tsp. lemon juice

⅓ cup wheat germ
pinch of paprika

Mix ingredients, adding a small amount of liquid if necessary to hold mixture together. Form into patties and pan fry in milk-free shortening.

Tuna Mousse

¼ cup cool water
2 tsp. gelatin, unflavored
1 cup hot water
1 Tbsp. chopped onion
    (optional)
1 tsp. lemon juice

½ tsp. dill weed
paprika (optional but helps
    color and flavor)
1 (6½ oz.) can tuna, drained
⅓ cup mayonnaise

In ¼ cup cool water, in a one-cup measure, sprinkle gelatin to soften (5 minutes). Then add very hot water to one-cup line and stir to dissolve gelatin. Pour gelatin, onion, lemon juice, dill and paprika in container of electric blender. Blend at high speed for 15 seconds. Turn off. Add flaked tuna and mayonnaise. Blend on high for 30 seconds, adding ⅓ cup more water if necessary to blend. Makes 2 cups of mixture which you can mold and chill in a small bowl or fancy shape mold till set. Serve on bread, crackers or plain lettuce and tomato.

Hint: Tuna mousse goes down easily when throats are sore or children are teething and can't chew.

Bread Crumbs

Instead of using a batter containing milk, try dipping fish, meat, or whatever, first in seasoned flour, then in egg beaten with a slight amount of water, then into your homemade milk-free bread crumbs. This can be done ahead and refrigerated till cooking time.

Variation: Kellogg's Corn Flake Crumbs work nicely here.

Yogurt Cheese

1 (8 oz.) container of plain yogurt
cheese cloth

In the evening, after the dinner dishes are done, spread out a 12-inch square double thickness of cheese cloth and place contents of yogurt container in the center. Bring four corners together, close and hang from the sink's water faucet overnight. In the morning remove the "cheese" from the cloth and refrigerate until ready to use. If yogurt is a food your child can tolerate, this recipe becomes a sort of cream cheese base for many spreads and dips.

The cheeses with the lowest lactose content are hard, aged cheeses such as Swiss and cheddar.

Milk-Free Desserts

Desserts don't have to be denied due to a lactose intolerance. In addition to fancy gelatins, parfaits made with non-dairy topping, fruits, peanut butter, granola, and frozen bananas covered with honey or peanut butter, there are many tempting traditional desserts to make.

Milk-Free Cake

(*Also known as Puddle Cake*)

1½ cups flour (white or half
    white, half whole wheat)
1 cup sugar
1 tsp. baking soda
1 tsp. vanilla

3 Tbsp. cocoa or carob
    powder
1 tsp. vinegar
6 Tbsp. cooking oil
1 cup water

Sift flour, sugar, soda and cocoa into an ungreased 8 x 10-inch cake pan. With a mixing spoon, make three holes in the dry mixture. Place vanilla in the first hole, vinegar in the second and oil in the third. Pour water over all and stir with a fork to moisten dry ingredients. Do not beat. Bake at 350° for 35 minutes.

"Margarine-Cream" Frosting

½ cup (1 stick) milk-free margarine
2 cups powdered sugar
1 egg yolk, well beaten
a drop of vanilla and/or ⅓ cup cocoa powder (not drink mix)

Cream margarine and sugar till very fluffy. Add egg yolk and beat. Then beat in vanilla and chocolate. For decorative frosting you can use vegetable shortening which will yield white instead of off-white frosting.

Unrestricted Peanut Butter Cookies

2 egg whites, slightly beaten
1 cup sugar

1½ cups peanut butter
½ cup toasted wheat germ
(optional)

Combine above ingredients and mix well. Drop by the teaspoon onto a lightly greased cookie sheet. Flatten gently with a fork. Bake 8-10 minutes at 350°.

Milk-Free Ice Cream

1 (8 oz.) container of
Richwhip® toppings,
thawed (or any non-dairy
eqivalent frozen liquid
whip topping)
¼ cup sugar or equivalent
sweetener
1 tsp. vanilla

⅓ cup cocoa powder
(not drink mix)
1 mashed banana
1 cup of
strawberries or
blueberries or any
favored fruit, fresh or
frozen (optional)

Whip the topping as you would heavy cream. When thickened, add sugar, vanilla and fruit. Freeze for ½ hour. Remove from freezer and beat for one minute. Pour into storage container, cover and freeze. Natural it is not (read ingredients listed on topping carton), but delicious and milk-free it is!

Hint: If eggs are not on the sensitive list, add one to the above recipe. Separate the egg. Add yolk to thickened "cream" but beat the egg white till almost stiff before folding into mixture.

Strawberry Ice

2 pkg. frozen sliced
    strawberries in syrup
⅓ cup ice water
¼ tsp. lemon juice

¼ cup orange juice, or omit
    water and use ¾ cup
    orange juice

Spin together in an electric blender till smooth. Turn off, scrape sides, blend again and pour into a plastic container. Cover and freeze until serving time. Makes 4-6 servings. Let stand at room temperature 5 minutes or so if mixture has frozen hard. You may want to add ½ cup honey or sugar when using two pints of fresh berries.

Home ice cream machines are excellent for making ices and milk-free ice cream style desserts.

Milk-Free Foods

Even though it may seem at times that all products contain milk and all recipes demand it, this is not really so. Here are some milk-free products that you'll be using. On packaged goods, it is important to always check the labels in case of reformulated recipes.

Milk and Milk Products

Coconut milk
Mayonnaise (such as Hellmann's/Best Foods)
Margarine (such as Fleischmann's margarine unsalted
    stick and diet Blue Bonnet margarine)

Bread and Grain Products

Rice
Pillsbury Crescent Rolls
Pita Bread
Sourdough bread and authentic French Bread
Crackers without milk products (such as Ritz Crackers,
    Keebler Town House Oval Crackers, Zesta Saltines,
    Nabisco Premium Saltine Crackers, Ry Krisp, Triscuits)
Tortillas

Sugar Products

Jams and Jellies
Carob
Chocoate (dark baking chocolate, semisweet morsels
    from Nestles and Hershey, and plain cocoa powder)
Duncan Hines cake mixes (many of them)
Baskin Robbins Fruit Ice
Gelatin desserts
Angel food cake
Sponge cake
Cool Whip (although this contains sodium caseinate)
Hard candies
Licorice
Marshmallows

Other

Meat, fish, poultry, eggs—prepared without milk products
Tofu
All vegetables without butter or cream sauces
Potatoes (but not instant potatoes to which lactose has
    been added during processing)
Pasta
Fruits (fresh, frozen or canned)
Chinese food (usually)
Kosher products, such as hot dogs (in kosher foods milk
    and meat are not combined)
Granola (not all brands)
Ketchup
Mustard
Relish
Peanut Butter
Campbell's Tomato Soup
Popcorn (unbuttered)
Cracker Jacks
Juices

In restaurants, fast food and otherwise, you'll not be able to let down your guard. Obviously you must avoid malts and shakes, but you must also watch out for creamed or breaded or batter dipped meat, fish or poultry. Also egg dishes made with milk, buttered vegetables, rolls and bread, salad dressings, creamed soups and chowders need to be avoided.

When your child goes to school or to a friend's house, send along a list to the person in charge of providing food indicating what your child can have. This would include fruits, fruit juice, meat, raisins, nuts, raw vegetables. State specifically the foods with milk included that cannot be eaten or ask that they call you. Most parents aren't aware of all the food products made with milk.

Make your life easier by:

- Stocking up on milk-free breads and freezing them in plastic bags.

- Preparing milk-free dishes for the freezer on a monthly basis.

- Finding a kosher bakery and stocking up on *pareve* items. Kosher cuisine can't mix milk and meat and the word *pareve* insures that there are no milk by-products.

- Packing a milk-free goody for your child when he or she will be out with friends.

- Ask your grocer to carry lactose-reduced milk.

Many companies will send you lists of their milk-free products. Here are three, for starters:

General Foods Consumer Center, Nutrition Services
250 North Street, White Plains, New York 10625

Nabisco, Inc. Consumer Services
East Hanover, New Jersey 07936

Ener-G Foods, Inc.
P.O. Box 84487, Seattle, Washington 98124

Your pediatrician may suggest adding small amounts of milk to your child's menu periodically. If the symptoms reappear, refrain from serving milk for another few months.

Cooking For Kids In a Microwave

If you have used a microwave oven you have learned what a terrific helper it is for a parent. Microwaves are safe (due to government regulations and fail-safe doors on ovens) convenient, fast and are easily affordable today. Microwaves can still cause burns—not from the microwave but from the steam released when covers are removed from microwaved food. Wear oven mitts and be sure to hold dishes away from your face when removed from oven. The questions are whether you have room in your kitchen and room in your budget. Standard ovens are being made with microwave units built in. A microwave is definitely a boon. It is one of the few true labor-saving devices on the market. Foods tend to cook quicker, reheat instantly and defrost when you've only begun to contemplate dinner at four in the afternoon. A microwave also saves the work of cleaning dishes that you would otherwise have to use because many foods can be prepared in their serving dishes. When you need to feed a family of six or more a microwave may not help your meal preparation as much as it will for a smaller family. The more you put into the microwave the longer it takes to cook.

A microwave can help you as a parent right from the beginning.

For Baby

You can heat a bottle in the microwave. It's important that you exert *extra* care. Milk or formula can heat faster than you expect and can scald a baby's mouth. Check carefully before serving.

Heating the bottle:

- one 8-ounce bottle at room temperature, 15-30 seconds.

- one 8-ounce bottle cold from the refrigerator, 30-60 seconds. (Remove nipple and screw cap before heating.)

Hint: Remember, however, that a cold bottle doesn't usually matter to the baby, only to the mother.

Heating baby food:

- Homemade frozen cubes or plops of pureed baby food can be warmed in approximately 60-90 seconds.

- A jar of baby food with cap removed can be warmed in approximately 30 seconds; a little longer when taken cold from the refrigerator. Three jars in a circle will heat in 90 seconds.

When buying commercial baby food, try to select from the basic fruits, vegetables and strained meats, avoiding combination meals and desserts.

Breakfast

Granola

Toasting granola in the microwave is fast and efficient. Because of the way it is uniformly heated, when it has cooled you find you have granola that is crunchy and lumpy instead of flaky.

3 cups uncooked oatmeal
1 cup untoasted wheat germ
1 cup unsweetened coconut
2 Tbsp. cinnamon
2 Tbsp. brown sugar

¼ cup powdered milk
⅓ cup honey
⅓ cup oil
1 tsp. vanilla

Mix all of the dry ingredients together in a large, shallow glass dish. Combine honey, oil and vanilla and heat in the microwave for 30 seconds. Drizzle this warm liquid over the dry ingredients, coating thoroughly, using your hands to stir. Place this mixture in your microwave for approximately 10-15 minutes. Cool completely before removing from dish and store in an airtight containter. (In a standard oven, toast at 250° for one hour or 300° for a half hour, stirring several times during the toasting process.)

Variation: Seeds, nuts, raisins or dates, when desired should be added after the mixture has cooled.

Oatmeal

¾ cup water
5 Tbsp. oatmeal (not the
    "Quick" kind)

1 tsp. brown sugar
1 Tbsp. butter
milk

Stir water and oatmeal together in a serving bowl. Microwave 1½ minutes. Stir, add butter, microwave until butter is melted. Remove from oven, add the sugar and as much milk as needed.

or

Make a large quantity of creamy old-fashioned oatmeal the night before, refrigerate, then reheat in individual serving dishes for breakfast the next day.

Pancakes and Waffles

A stack of pancakes made ahead can be reheated in a matter of seconds. Waffles reheat even more quickly.

Muenster Soup

Microwave a hunk of favorite cheese (my kids prefer Muenster but any will work) in a cereal bowl till just melted. Serve with a spoon, and either crackers or toast!

Bacon

Bacon is a fatty, though delicious, food that can be cooked so easily in a microwave. (But should be served infrequently.) Put two or three layers of paper toweling on the bottom of a glass serving dish. Lay your bacon on this, then cover with two more layers of paper toweling. Microwave for 1-2 minuties for 4-6 slices. Timing depends on the quantity of bacon you are cooking and your personal taste. The bacon browns nicely, the grease is absorbed by the toweling, and you have not splattered your stovetop.

Hint: Divide up your package of bacon into serving sizes and freeze.

Lunch

Hot Swiss Tuna On Buns

1 can tuna, drained
1 cup shredded Swiss or
    Cheddar cheese
¼ cup mayonnaise

1 tsp. lemon juice
4 hamburger buns
Chopped olives or sweet
    relish (optional)

Combine tuna, mayonnaise, lemon juice and shredded cheese. Divide mixture among the four buns and place them in the microwave on a paper towel, leaving space between the buns. Microwave for 60-90 seconds. Cheese heats quickly in a microwave. Seconds make a difference. You know it is overcooked when it is rubbery.

Hot Dogs On A Stick

Insert a popsicle stick in the end of a hot dog and cook on a paper plate. Again a meal that should be an occasional rather than a daily affair.

1 frankfurter, a little over half-a-minute
2 frankfurters, 60-90 seconds
5 frankfurters, 2-3 minutes

Hamburgers

Shape one pound of ground beef into four patties. Coat with soy sauce or basting sauce to "brown" burger. Place on a 9-inch glass pie plate or square baking dish. Cover with waxed paper, paper plate or towel and cook approximately 3 minutes. Turn hamburgers and rotate the dish. Cook 3 minutes longer until the patties are done. Hamburgers should not be overdone. Like most meats, they continue to cook after removal from the oven.

Melted Cheese Sandwich

2 slices whole wheat bread, preferable frozen slices of
    cheese (Muenster, Cheddar, Swiss and others)

Place cheese slices between bread slices. Put on a paper plate and microwave for 30 seconds or until cheese starts to melt. Let cool, cut in halves or quarters, and serve.

Variation: Use tortillas instead of bread which you then roll up when the cheese is soft or melted. These are called *quesadillas*.

Lazybones Applesauce

4 cooking apples
2 Tbsp. sweetener
cinnamon to taste (optional)

Place 4 clean, cored, apples on a glass baking dish. Microwave 6-8 minutes until apples are soft. Let cool. Peel off skin or scrape soft insides from apple skin into glass dish. Mash with a fork. Add sweetener, if needed, and cinnamon, if desired.

Dinner

Baked Potatoes

Baking potatoes in almost no time at all is one of the microwave oven's best accomplishments. When you find it easier to bake potatoes than to heat the frozen French fries, you will surely serve this tasty vegetable—rich in vitamin C, iron and many other vitamins and minerals—in its more wholesome form oftener than its fattier, more processed "relative."

To cook: Use medium-sized potatoes, scrub them well and prick several times with a fork. Arrange on a paper towel or paper plate. If you have several potatoes, arrange them in a circle with at least one inch of space between each, and bake as follows:

1 potato, 3-4 minutes
2 potatoes, 5-6 minutes
3 potatoes, 8-9 minutes
4 potatoes, 10-11 minutes
5 potatoes, 13-15 minutes

The larger the potato the longer it will take to cook. Potatoes continue to cook after they are removed from the oven and they keep hot for quite a long time.

Serve with milk and low fat margarine. Go easy on the butter and sour cream.

Time Saving Meatloaf

1 cup of croutons
½ cup milk
1 egg
2 tsp. Worcestershire sauce

¼ cup chopped onions
1 pound ground beef
ketchup or chili sauce

Let croutons stand in milk in a bowl for 5 minutes. Add egg, Worcestershire sauce and onions and mix well. Add ground beef. Press mixture into an ungreased glass loaf dish. Make a groove down the middle of the loaf and fill with ketchup. Microwave on high for 6 minutes. Rotate and cook another 5 minutes. Pour off excess juices and oil and cook another two minutes. Let it stand a few minutes before serving.

Vegetables

Vegetables cooked by microwave need little or no water, which makes the oven the most exciting vegetable cooker to arrive on the market so far. All the nutrition stays in the vegetables until you eat them. When cooking vegetable, a general time rule would be 6-8 minutes (stirring once or twice) for four servings in a covered dish. However, some vegetables—frozen peas, for instance—can be microwaved in individual small cups for 30-60 seconds.

Beware Of Micro-steam

Steam released when covers are taken off microwaved foods can cause serious burns. Wear oven mittens and hold microwave dishes away from your face when opening them.

Spaghetti Squash

If you have not tried this vegetable before, you should now. A spaghetti squash looks like a normal, hard-skinned yellow squash but it is different once it is cooked. The easiest way to cook it is to puncture it a few times with a knife (to let the steam escape) and put it in the microwave for 10 to 20 minutes or until the squash feels a bit soft to the touch. Let it cool; cut it in half and scoop out the center seeds with a spoon. Now use a fork to scoop out the squash meat and it will come out in strands and look just like spaghetti. Serve it with a pat of butter, grated cheese or even spaghetti sauce! Kids love it.

Corn-On-The-Cob

When cooking corn in the microwave you can either remove the outer husks and silk and wrap each individual corn ear in a paper towel or you can simply open the fresh corn, remove the silk and rewrap it in the outer husks. One ear of corn takes approximately 2 minutes and two ears, 4 minutes.

Micro Desserts

Desserts are not one of the stronger areas where a microwave is useful. (Maybe this fact makes it the perfect oven!) Cakes cook lumpishly, can scorch and require repeated turning during the baking period. Pastry will not brown but you can give it color by adding 1 teaspoon of cocoa or instant coffee to the flour.

Baked Apple

1 apple	¼ tsp. cinnamon
1 Tbsp. butter	½ tsp. brown sugar

Core and peel skin from the top of each apple. A single apple can be baked in a ceramic or glass dish. Fill the center of each apple with butter, sugar and cinnamon. Cook, uncovered, in the microwave 3-4 minutes for one apple, 5-7 minutes for two, 8-10 for four. Before serving you may wish to top them with a little milk, cream or ice cream.

Hint: Instead of butter and sugar, pour defrosted apple juice frozen concentrate into the center of each apple.

Pineapple Upside-Down Cake

2 Tbsp. butter or margarine	½ cup walnut halves
¼ cup packed brown sugar	(optional)
1 (8 oz.) can sliced pineapple,	2 tsp. baking powder
drained, which has been	⅓ cup powdered milk
packed in its own juice (or	½ cup cooking oil
well drained, crushed	1 egg
pineapple)	1 tsp. vanilla
1⅓ cup flour	½ cup of drained pineapple
1 cup sugar	juice

Melt butter and brown sugar in an 8-inch round or square glass pan. Microwave 1 minute. Smooth mixture evenly over bottom of pan. Add drained pineapple (reserve the liquid) and nuts, if using. Combine balance of ingredients. Pour batter over pineapple mixture and spread evenly and gently. Microwave 8 to 10 minutes, turning pan often. If the center still looks moist, microwave another 2 minutes. Remove from the oven and let cool 1 minute before turning out on a platter. Serve hot or cool, with or without a creamy topping.

Peachy Delight

1 peach half
¼ tsp. butter
1 tsp. brown sugar

Put butter and brown sugar inside the peach half and microwave 1 minute for one, 2 minutes for two, and 3 minutes for four peach halves.

Caramel Bananas

Warm a tablespoon of butter and a tablespoon of maple syrup together in a dish for 20-30 seconds. Coat a peeled banana in this mixture and then heat it for one minute in the microwave. Serve with a dash of lemon juice.

Micro Snacks

Unpizza Snack

In a mug place a spoonful of spaghetti sauce and a hunk of cheese (probably Mozzarella). Heat 60 seconds or until the cheese melts and eat with a spoon.

Wise Crax

Melt cheese on a graham cracker.

Cheesie Chippies

Toss taco chips with a cup or two of grated American cheese and microwave until the cheese melts.

Talking about cheese—a slice of American, or any variety, placed on a Sloppy Joe, tuna sandwich, egg salad, etc., and microwaved 30 seconds will help prevent the filling from spilling.

Micro Drinks

No longer must you wait forever for the frozen orange juice you forgot to take out the night before to defrost in time for breakfast. After removing the top, place the can in the microwave oven for 30-60 seconds. (This is assuming that the whole can is not made out of metal.) Mix with water as directed on the can and serve at once.

Hot Chocolate

Fill a plastic or ceramic cup three-quarters full with milk. Add 1 to 2 tablespoons cocoa mix or carob drink mix. Marshmallows are optional (mighty optional). Microwave 1-2 minutes and stir when removed from oven. The neat thing is that you can make hot chocolate with milk because it will not scorch. No need to use the envelope mixes that contain dry milk as well as many other ingredients which are not necessary.

Hot Apple Juice With Cinnamon

Fill glass, ceramic or plastic mug with apple juice, insert a cinnamon stick or dash of cinnamon and heat in the microwave for 1 minute.

Let The Kids Do The Cooking

The microwave is a terrific oven for your children to use. As soon as they are old enough to understand directions (around 5 or 6 years of age) they can help prepare many foods themselves. They can try recipes such as hot dogs, grilled cheese sandwiches or making their own hot drink. Children will not burn themselves on the oven because a microwave never gets hot. Nor does the dish; only the food.

Browning plates are becoming more popular with the use of microwaves. They brown the food they cook by becoming super hot themselves. A browning plate might be dangerous for a young child to use as he or she could be burned.

Picnics

Microwave hot dogs, hamburgers, and corn-on-the-cob at home. Then wrap these in aluminum foil and pack in your picnic basket. The food will stay hot quite a while.

Fast Food Restaurants

If your spouse has just brought home dinner from a fast food restaurant, the whole bag (cold drinks removed, of course) can be inserted in the microwave oven and reheated a few minutes (assuming none of the foods are wrapped in aluminum foil). Or, if you prefer, simply put individual servings on plates and microwave each plate, one at a time, approximately 30-60 seconds.

When using the microwave oven it is better to set the time on the low side a second or two than to risk overcooking your food.

Fringe Benefits

- *To soften butter*: Place stick of butter or margarine in a glass measuring cup or non-metallic mixing bowl. Heat 10 seconds, let stand 10 seconds. Repeat till shortening reaches required softness.

- *To soften raisins*: Pour a little water over 2 cups raisins. Heat uncovered 2 minutes, let stand 2 minutes. Drain and use.

- *To roast raw peanuts*: Place 3 cups of raw peanuts which have been tossed with 1 Tbsp. oil in a shallow baking dish. Microwave for 15 to 20 minutes, stirring nuts every 2 minutes. You must let them cool before tasting as they will still seem "raw" when warm.

- *To roast chestnuts*: Make an X slash in each of 18-24 chestnuts. Place them in a single layer on an appropriate dish. Microwave (uncovered) for 1 minute. Turn the nuts and microwave another minute. Stir nuts one last time and microwave for another minute. If done, they will be soft when squeezed. Let them cool 5 minutes before peeling to eat.

- *To empty containers*: To really empty many containers such as honey or ketchup, heat until more "liquidy" and pour out.

- *To clarify honey*: Clarify honey turned to sugar by heating jar without cap for 1 minute.

- *To warm foods*: Foods can be warmed in (and the warmth retained) in a small wide-mouth *all plastic* thermos container.

- *To soften brown sugar*: Place bag of sugar in microwave for 30-60 seconds.

HINT: For mom or dad, save leftover tea or coffee in glass jars. Refrigerate, then reheat as needed.

I'VE JUST GOT A FEW THINGS
FOR YOU TO REMEMBER WHILE
I'M OUT....

Sitter Selections ...Food That Is

Getting a sitter, getting the kids ready and yourself together—not to mention having dinner done ahead—can make preparing for your evening out an exhausting experience. The following information on what to prepare ahead to feed your kids and the sitter will help with one aspect of getting yourself out of the house on time.

You may catch yourself spitting out a slew of instructions to your sitter as he or she walks in the door. If any instructions are overlooked, it will probably be because a sitter can absorb only so much information per second. If it is important—write it down.

When your child is small it is important to be specific about what you want your sitter to do. Write it down. Let the sitter know when to expect sleeping, waking, crying and eating. Point out the diapers and your child's favorite diversions. If you expect the baby to be held while being fed from a bottle and burped every three ounces, say so; better yet, write it down. Get the bib out, the food (if appropriate), spoon and any other necessary items so that the sitter will not have to search. If you have an infant, you should have something ready for your sitter to eat that requires little or no preparation, with an alternative that the sitter can make if he or she really doesn't like what you've left. (See my *Dear Babysitter Handbook* for additional ideas, fill-in forms and first aid information.)

When your children are older, the sitter will probably eat with them. Such meals should require minimum preparation—you want your sitter to keep an eye on the children, not on the stove. (You know the problem you have when you're making dinner!) While your sitters may have more cooking knowledge than you give them credit for, you should keep the menu simple. But don't leave it open-ended. Make specific suggestions if you have not made a meal ahead of time. Tell your sitter where to find the basics he or she may need. Your sitter doesn't know your cupboards like you do.

If you don't want your kids eating sweets or snacks, name your restrictions. You may need to do this for the sitter as well. When the cake you baked for tomorrow's bridge party is off limits, better say so.

The most common sitter fare seems to be peanut butter sandwiches, pizza or macaroni and cheese. (And you thought you were the only one!) One way to add variety is with some good freeze-to-please meals, easy to heat or reheat. No doubt you have your favorite casserole dishes, or try these. Actually, why wait for the sitter?

French Toast

French toast is a good way to combine eggs, milk and bread. If you use homemade or whole grain bread, you will have to handle it more carefully. These breads are more fragile than white bread after being soaked in the mixture, and break more easily.

Here are two batter recipes:

1 egg		1 egg
⅓ cup milk	or	4 tsp. flour
⅛ tsp. vanilla		⅓ cup milk

The above batters are each enough for approximately 3 slices of bread. For both recipes beat the eggs lightly and add the next two ingredients. Dip bread in mixture and fry in a well greased pan over fairly high heat, browning well on both sides. Or, on a cold morning you can preheat the oven to 500° and bake the dipped bread on a greased pan, turning after the top browns.

For quick freezing place French toast on a cookie sheet and put in the freezer for a half hour. Remove from the freezer, place in freezer bags and seal well. The advantage of freezing the pieces separately is that they will not stick together in the freezer bag. When ready to use, your babysitter can place the pieces of toast in an oven toaster or regular toaster for a quick main course.

Macaroni Salad

1 cup elbow macaroni	½ cup diced celery
4 cups water	½ cup grated carrots
½ cucumber, diced	½ cup mayonnaise
2 sliced, hard-cooked eggs	1 tsp. lemon juice
½ cup diced cheese	

Cook macaroni in 4 cups of boiling water according to directions on package. Drain and chill. Stir in other ingredients including mayonnaise and lemon juice combined. This will serve 2 hungry children and one babysitter as well.

Hamburger Heroes

⅔ cup evaporated milk	1 egg
1 lb. lean ground beef	½ cup chopped onion
½ cup bread or cracker crumbs, or untoasted wheat germ	1 tsp. prepared mustard
	1 cup grated cheese
⅛ tsp. pepper	a loaf of French bread

Mix all the filling ingredients together. There will be enough to make 1 large or 2 small hero sandwiches. Cut the French bread loaf in half lengthwise. Spread the filling on cut side of each half. Wrap foil around the crusts of the bread halves, leaving the filling uncovered, and bake on a cookie sheet in a preheated oven at 350° for 25 minutes. Envelop heroes completely in foil when they are to be refrigerated for future use.

Before serving, garnish with cheese strips, mushrooms, olives, peppers, etc. Cut large hero loaves in slices. Smaller loaves may be offered half-a-loaf to a customer.

Hint: Meatloaf is another food variation that's easy to make ahead.

Pizza

Jazz up a frozen pizza with extra cheese, meat or spices, or make your own pizza.

Pizza crust

Frozen Bread Dough Recipe for a Thick Pizza Crust

Roll or press out one thawed frozen bread dough to fit a round pizza plate or oblong pan. Pinch edges to form a rim. Prick with a fork and brush with oil. Bake at 400° till light brown (about 10 minutes). Freeze crust for future use or add toppping and bake at 400° till cheese melts. (Although the frozen French bread dough is good to use, try a darker bread for a nutritious change.)

Make Your Own Regular Pizza Crust:

1⅓ cups warm water
1 pkg. dry yeast
2 Tbsp. salad oil
2 tsp. salt
4⅓ cups flour (white or half
    white, half whole wheat)

Dissolve yeast in water. Add oil, salt and flour. Knead for 10 minutes. Put dough in a lightly oiled bowl and cover with a damp cloth. Place in a warm place to rise till doubled in size. Punch down. Divide into two balls. Roll or press out into pizza shape. This recipe provides enough dough for two crusts. Bake both pizzas (400° about 10 min.) and freeze one or both, as you choose.

Yes, you can purchase a shelf-stable, packaged pizza crust mix at your grocery store, too!

Pizza topping

Lightly cover the crust with oil and add a layer of tomato sauce (approximately 1 cup), grated cheese (Mozzarella, Swiss, Monterey Jack or whatever), spices.

Options: cooked sausage, olives, green pepper, mushrooms, onion, crumbled cooked hamburger, sliced tomatoes or any leftovers.

More cheese (such as grated Parmesan) on top. Bake at 400° for 10-20 minutes till cheese melts.

Tuna Baked Biscuits

1 (7 oz.) can of tuna, drained
   and flaked
⅓ cup mayonnaise
¼ cup diced celery

1 small carrot, grated
2 Tbsp. sweet relish
1 pkg. (10) refrigerated
   biscuits

Mix first five ingredients. Separate biscuits. On a lightly floured surface, roll them into the shape of a flat pancake. Spoon tuna salad onto 5 of the circles (or 4, if you prefer a heftier sandwich). Top with remaining circles. Seal by pressing around the edges with fork. Put on an ungreased baking sheet at 375° for 15 minutes or until browned. These can be served warm or cold from the refrigerator. They can also be frozen. To serve, defrost and toast in toaster oven or large oven for a few minutes.

Almost Fried Chicken

There's always chicken…yours, the Colonel's or the grocery's frozen fried variety. (Nutritionally speaking, boiled is better, but you might lose your babysitter.)

¼ cup cornmeal
½ tsp. garlic powder
8 chicken legs
1 egg white

¼ tsp. Tabasco
¼ cup bran or corn flakes,
   crushed

Preheat oven to 350°. Combine cornmeal and garlic and sprinkle over washed chicken legs. Mix egg white and Tabasco. Dip each leg in the mixture, then roll in flakes. Bake 20 minutes until crisp.

Mexican Chili Casserole

1 (15 oz.) can chili
1 (12 or 17 oz.) can whole
   kernel corn

1 (8 oz.) pkg. grated cheese
1 to 2 cups crumbed corn or
   nacho chips (or 7½ oz. bag)

Combine chili, drained corn and grated cheese. Crumble chips over the top of the casserole, pressing them gently into the mixture. Bake at 350° for 20 minutes. Serve casserole with extra whole chips.

Pasties

(A meal-all-in-one! A portable pot pie!)

Pasty dough

2 cups flour	1 Tbsp. lemon juice
2 tsp. baking powder	1 egg yolk, unbeaten
1 tsp. salt	½ cup hot water
⅔ cup shortening	

Combine flour, baking powder and salt. Cut shortening into mixture. Add lemon juice, egg yolk and hot water and mix well. Divide dough into 4-5 round balls.

Hint: Defrosted frozen bread dough works well here. Roll a piece of dough into an 8 x 6-inch rectangle. Add ½ cup of filling on one half and fold over the remaining half of the dough and seal the edges well.

Pasty filling

1 lb. round steak, diced	1 large onion, chopped
½ lb. pork steak, diced	4-5 diced carrots
5-6 medium-sized potatoes, diced	seasonings

On a floured surface, roll a ball of the pasty dough into a circle. Place a handful of filling onto one-half of the circle. Top with a dot of butter. Fold dough over (as for a turnover) and crimp edges. Prick top of crust. Bake at 400° for 20 minutes, then at 350° for 40 minutes until juice dries up around pasty.

For freezing, bake a little less. Wrap in foil. Leave in foil to reheat.

Hint: This is not a quickie recipe. You can split up the preparation time by dicing the filling ingredients prior to making the pasties (such as the day before). Either way, they are well worth the effort!

Using paper plates when sitters are over may well make everyone happier. If you expect dishes rinsed or put in the dishwasher or put away, you will have to specify. Sitters don't enjoy doing dishes any more than you do!

Homemade TV Dinners

Make your own TV dinner dishes—use the aluminum dishes, or others with divided compartments. Fill with:

Main Course (precooked)	Vegetables	Other
hot dog	peas	garlic bread
hamburger	carrots	roll
macaroni and cheese	corn	cooked rice
your child's favorite hot dish	squash	cooked noodles
	mashed potatoes	

Cook fresh vegetables or repack the trays from bags of the frozen variety.

Let the babysitter pull out the appropriate number of trays before mealtime to heat in the oven for 20-40 minutes at 350°.

Eating En Route

Summer vacation! Visit to grandma! The long planned cross-country trip! Whether traveling by car, bus or plane, eating will be a major activity (or trauma) on any trip. No matter what games or activities you plan, food will be the star attraction. Be prepared! Food requests often come within 15 minutes of leaving your driveway, closely following the question, "*Are we there yet?*"

Save time by referring to the following list before you begin your trip. Despite the convenience of convenience foods while traveling, good-for-you foods are as easy to carry and more enjoyable to eat.

Proteins

Hard-cooked eggs in the shell
Cheeses (bite-sized), such as wrapped Gruyere sections, and curds
Nuts
Peanut butter balls (see page 21)
A jar of peanut butter
A roll of salami (not advisable on a bus or airplane if you wish to remain in the good grace of your fellow travelers)
Cooked cold chicken
Yogurt containers served with a straw through the top lid

Note: Avoid sandwich spreads made with mayonnaise if you are not carrying a cooler. Unrefrigerated, they spoil quickly.

Fruits and Vegetables

Apples (cored to save waste and mess, good stuffed with
    peanut butter or soft cheese)
Pears (can be cored also)
Seedless grapes
Raisins
Fruit leather, homemade or commercial
Dried apple rings (see page 47)
Bananas (never pack at the bottom of your bag!)
Navel oranges (pre-cut or skin pre-scored)
Carrot and celery sticks (immersed in cold water for a
    long trip—otherwise just washed and packed in a
    plastic bag)

Etc...Etc...Etc.

Finger Jell-O™ (see page 46. Can go unrefrigerated four hours)
Soft pretzels (less crumbly than other kinds)
Packaged granola bars
Popcorn (in small individual bags)
Gorp...a mixture of nuts, raisins and chocolate chips
Pepperidge Farm Fish Crackers
Small boxes of dry cereal (see page 122 for instructions
    on how to calculate which brands have lower sugar content)

Crackers are usually crumbly, especially saltines. Nevertheless, a
fun and easy snack for traveling is a box of crackers (try Wheat Thins
or Triscuits) and a bottle of squirt cheese. Squirt cheese, while not
recommended as standard fare—can be very appropriate for traveling. Mom or Dad can dispense the cheese on the crackers in designs,
letters or numbers.

Bagels are the least crumbly travelers, ideal for sandwiches when
sliced and filled with cream cheese, sliced cheese, or peanut butter.

Drinks

One wise mother I know of carried only water—ice cold water—
when traveling. Spilled, it wasn't sticky. Nor did it stain. Since water

appealed less than sweetened drinks, it was requested less frequently and subsequent "potty stops" were fewer.

Other drink ideas:

- Small individual cans or boxes of juice can be frozen beforehand and allowed to thaw along the way.

- Those lovely Airpots travel well and make accidents more easily avoidable when dispensing drinks. (They must travel in an upright position.)

- Tupperware plastic glasses with spill-proof lids are terrific travelers for drink or food. Or just fill them with ice cubes to melt enroute for cold water.

- A camper canteen can be an exciting and personal drinking container.

- Fill a plastic juice-type container half-way with water and then freeze it. Remove from freezer and fill it to the top with water. The water will stay cold all day as the block of ice melts slowly.

- Recycle your plastic lemon or lime juice containers. Empty the juice concentrate, remove the insert (try an ice pick), rinse and fill with water or juice. Replace insert. Children can squirt the liquid into their mouths with a minumum of drip. Put cap on to close and prevent leaking.

- Clear soft drinks that don't stain when spilled.

- FORGET MILK! It is not easy on the tummy when traveling.

Meal Ideas

One of the nicest ways to eat en route is to picnic. Food for easy-to-make roadside picnics can either be brought or purchased in grocery stores along the way. At a picnic the service is always speedy. No tipping is required. Children are free to roam and to get needed exercise. Maybe you can even find a park with a playground.

Car meals are best controlled by keeping the food container next to the non-driving parent. Food dispensed one course at a time helps pass the hours and keeps down the mess.

An empty shoe box makes a good lap tray.

Sandwiches are easier for children to handle when made on cock-tail-sized breads.

If you need a quick breakfast to get you on the road early, bring along a cold breakfast cereal mixed with powdered milk (approximately 2 Tbsp. powdered milk to one cup cereal.) Serve in paper cups or paper bowls. Add water and you have an INSTANT BREAKFAST. Don't forget the spoons.

Fast-Food Restaurants

For most people, eating en route means stopping at fast-food restaurants. Their speed is a blessing to parents of hungry children with short attention spans, but nutritional balance is wanton. These restaurants supply ample protein accompanied by excess calories from frying (French fries) and sugars (sodas and shakes). Missing are the nutrients of fruits and vegetables. This is the best argument for buying burgers with lettuce, tomato and onion.

The typical fast-food meal is not devoid of food value; rather, it is somewhat unbalanced. One hundred percent of your FDA carbohydrate (sugar and starch) daily need will be met, but little of your vitamin C need, for instance.

Most of us can get nearly half our day's calorie requirement from one meal at a fast-food restaurant. And when traveling by car there is no opportunity to work it off. High fat, low fiber meals accompanied by little exercise are just not healthful. So supplement! Don't hesitate to bring some fruits or vegetables from your car or your home. Apples, for one, fit easily into pockets. Avoid French fries as a side dish. Also, patronize those restaurants that provide salad bars and baked potatoes. Buy milk for a better balanced meal instead of colas or chocolate shakes. Or buy juice where available. Look for water fountains and ask for glasses of water.

If you want to find out what you're really eating, check out *The Fast Food Guide: What's Good, What's Bad And How To Tell The Difference*, by Michael Jacobsen, director of Center for Science in the Public Interest (CSPI) and nutritionist, Sarah Fritschner (Workman, 1986). This guidebook enables eaters to make choices about fast foods.

You may have heard that fast food chains are moving to disclose the ingredient and nutrient content of their meals. You can receive nutrition booklets by writing to: **McDonald's** Nutrition Information Center, McDonald's Plaza, Oak Brook, Illinois 60521; **Wendy's** International, Inc., Consumer Affairs Department, P.O. Box 256, Dublin, Ohio 43017; **Burger King** Corporation, Consumer Relations Department, Mail Station 1490, Miami, Florida 33152. Though the information is sparse and hard to use comparatively, you can learn that the sodium content of shakes is higher than that of french fries, and that McDonald's now offers low-fat milk.

Fast-food chains are growing in popularity as evidenced by their appearance at every available corner. They can be part of eating en route, but not the major part if we wish to have a balanced diet. If you wish to maintain a clean car (good luck!), avoid eating at drive-in restaurants. Also you don't get the chance to stretch!

If sit-down restaurants are part of your travel plans, you may want to make some pre-trip, eat out, practice jaunts. Remembering to avoid arrival at traditional meal hours may save long waits and jumpy children. The same children who crave food constantly while traveling in a car may not finish their plate in a restaurant.

Don't rule out hotel/motel room service. Occasionally, despite expense, the advantages and convenience may be well worthwhile. Or plan your own picnic in your room and let the kids enjoy their meal in the bathtub, which makes for a quick clean up.

For additional food and travel tips, you may wish to refer to my book, *Trouble-Free Travel with Children (Book Peddlers, 1991)*.

WAIT! One last thing before you go. Consider these other bring-alongs:

Plastic bags—for garbage, motion sickness, dirty laundry, for storing foods, toys, wet bathing suits, souvenirs, etc.

Disposable moist towelettes—for clean-up (a damp wash cloth in a plastic bag serves the same purpose).

Sugar-free gum—or one small package of hard candies to settle a stomach, keep ears from popping in an airplane, as a hold-over in a slow serving restaurant.

To Market
—a Selective Guide For Parents

Shopping in a grocery store is a function performed by one, if not both parents, at least once a week. Each week we consider what we can get for our food dollar, what we can get in nutritional value, and what we can get that is appetizing both for ourselves and our families. There is no one in the grocery store to guide us through, or to tell us which foods meet each need we must give thought to. Much of the food in the grocery store has been placed there by food processors who derive large profits from their packaged edibles. It is necessary to shop armed with knowledge—and a calculator wouldn't hurt—to get the best for our money.

THE MOST HEALTHFUL WAY TO SHOP IN YOUR SUPER-MARKET IS TO SHOP ONLY THE PERIPHERY OF THE STORE.

The most wholesome and necessary foods are nearly all located in the outer aisles. There you will find dairy products, meats, produce, frozen foods, and probably the bakery area. Actually, you miss little by not going up and down the middle aisles, but we are conditioned to do this. Keep in mind that the dairy case is purposely set in the farthest corner to make sure you continue through the store.

The miracle of the modern distribution system is not convenience, as the major food companies would have you believe, but that you can eat bananas all year long that are grown in far away countries· that eggs are always available without your having to raise chickens; that those in the northern United States, where oranges don't grow and most crops are harvested in the fall, can eat fresh citrus fruit every day to insure adequate vitamin C intake.

Ideally, you should shop alone. (Good luck!) More often you are racing through the store before the baby awakens, or bribing your offspring to behave with food treats, or constantly berating them, "Do not touch. Stop running. No, you can't have that." Or is this the day your little one decides to have a tantrum in the grocery store?

Why shop alone? So that you can read labels, compare prices, and not be coaxed into buying items you don't need. Since it is impractical to assume that you can do this all the time, it is important to do so every once in a while. I'm sure that it will have an invaluable carry-over when you must shop with tots in tow.

What should you look for when you do get a chance to read labels? Primarily SUGAR! Sugar listed as the first ingredient means that there is more sugar in that package than any other single ingredient. Try to buy products where sugar is specified at least third, if not fourth or fifth, on the label. This is not always significant however; while sugar might not be named first, you could find any of five additional sweeteners listed such as brown sugar, honey, molasses, dextrose and corn syrups. Food companies often combine the grains on labels but split the sugars, listing each type separately. Then sugar does not appear as the first ingredient.

Look to see where salt falls on the list of ingredients. The farther down the list, the better. While it is next to impossible to avoid salt, you will at least see why nutritionists and doctors are so concerned about our excessive salt consumption. You might be spurred to make more dishes from scratch without salt when you realize how abundantly it is used in packaged foods. It is in diet soft drinks, canned tuna, canned vegetables, mayonnaise (list of ingredients not required), and grated Parmesan cheese, to name a few.

Choose, when possible, "enriched white flour" over "flour." The latter is often listed as "wheat flour."

Also try to avoid hardened (hydrogenated) fats. They are harder to digest.

Choose natural flavorings over artificial flavorings whenever possible. Generally, the fewer chemical additives in food the better off you will be. Natural flavorings are often more expensive than artificial (synthetic) ones, which is why they are less commonly used. Food colorings (found most frequently in soda, candy, gelatin mixes, pudding mixes, cereals, ice cream and other snack foods) are needed in manufactured foods to imply richness and flavor to the eye. While most additives are safe, they do make less wholesome foods appear more wholesome and appetizing.

Let's take a short trip down grocery store lane rethinking what we see there every week, looking for the best in food value, particularly for the small children in our households. If your favorite foods are skipped over, forgive me. Some have been skipped on purpose, others not.

Produce

Let's start with the produce section, usually near the entrance anyway.

Bananas

When you buy them green, wait until they are yellow and ripe before eating. Bananas can be bought on special (which means they are ripe) and used for banana bread, milk shakes or popsicles. You can slice and freeze them for later baking uses. Usually three bananas equal one pound.

Apples

One of the best fall, winter and spring fruits which most children enjoy. They are good plain, baked, dried and sauced. Try serving half-an-apple on a popsicle stick. The best gadget I ever purchased is an apple corer that removes the center easily, going a long way to eliminate waste by children who never eat close to the core. And there is an apple cutter on the market that cuts an apple into eight sections with one downward push.

Oranges

While squeeze-it-yourself orange juice is certainly best because the pulp also provides important food value, you may opt for the frozen variety since it is inexpensive, convenient, and there is no sugar added. To provide the food value of the pulp, do serve eating oranges regularly. Navel oranges have few or no seeds. Instead of slicing them in quarters, for a change cut them in 1/4 inch slices so you have orange circles. Oranges are often artificially colored so don't be put off by oranges with a green tinge. They are fine!

Pears

If they are too firm when you buy them, let them sit on your counter a few days to soften, then refrigerate.

Peaches

Look for good peach tones, not green tones, when peaches are in season.

Cantaloupe

This summer fruit is tops in taste and food value. A ripe cantaloupe usually smells as good as it tastes, which is usually at the height of its season when it is most plentiful. Serve it wedged or cubed, morning or night.

Watermelon

This summer fruit is another good-for-you melon. For ripeness, look for a flattish yellow side. Young children usually like (or need) pits removed. If you cube it, remove the pits. Whir it in a blender and then freeze it in popsicle forms for a treat.

Berries

These were invented just the right size for children and most children love them. Serve with toothpicks, or in cream, or combined with other fruits.

Grapes

Green seedless are favored by most. You may want to cut them in half for very young children to insure that they are eaten and not just swallowed whole (or choked on). A small plastic bag is a good container for a bunch of grapes.

Kiwi

Surely by now you have tried this delicious and nutritious green fruit. It comes with a fuzzy brown skin and a soft, sweet green inside. You can cut off the brown skin and then slice it in circles for a finger food, or slice a kiwi in half and eat it as you would a small melon.

Pineapple

Should smell as fresh as it looks. There should be a yellow blush on the skin, and the leaves should be dark green.

Carrots

Unless they are very scruffy looking, carrots need not be peeled. A good scrub is sufficient. If you puree them for a infant, peel to remove bacteria or insect parts which might hang on. Carrots are more digestible when they are cooked soft, though children as they grow older tend to prefer carrots raw. Short on time? Slice them before cooking.

Cucumbers

Usually waxed for transporting so you may wish to use your carrot peeler here. The largest ones don't always taste the best. If you grow your own, do leave the green skin on. If you need to remove the seeds to have them eaten, do so.

Potatoes

White potatoes are rich in minerals and vitamins, including vitamin C. A medium-sized potato has about the same number of calories as a large apple. Potatoes baked or boiled in their jackets are more nutritious than those French-fried. Sweet potatoes and yams offer the same plus a lot of vitamin A and more fiber. No potato, white or yellow, should be stored in the refrigerator as the excess coolness can change its texture.

St. Patrick's Potatoes

Combine mashed potatoes, pureed broccoli, a bit of milk and grated Parmesan cheese in honor of that holiday!

Lettuces

All varieties may not be preferred but they are all a good source of fiber. Iceberg offers the least nutrients but is often preferred over others with a stronger taste and texture.

Green vegetables

Broccoli, asparagus, zucchini, etc.—all of which are excellent for you. (My son won't touch any green vegetables with the exception of artichokes dipped in butter sauce.) Most can be served raw with a dip as well as steamed or baked.

This could continue but I'll stop here so we may move on through the "store."

In Cans and Jars

Applesauce

Natural style applesauce contains apples and water only. It is found in the same section as applesauces which contain added sugar, and sometimes salt and citric acid. Do check the label. Natural apple-sauce may be priced higher but it is the better buy.

Fruits

Try to select canned fruits packed in light syrup rather than heavy. Heavy syrup means heavy with sugar. Light syrup has less sugar. Some fruits are packed in their own juice without extra sugar added.

Tuna fish

Probably our most popular canned fish. The kind of fish that goes into the can varies and so does the price. The term "white meat" designates the whitest, fanciest and most expensive. "Light meat" is a combination of fish similar in color and flavor that serves as a versa-tile all purpose choice for less money. Solid packs cost more because they consist of more pieces. Chunked tuna in smaller pieces costs less and still cheaper is flaked or grated, all fine for sandwiches or casseroles. Supermarket or private brands or unadvertised brands are usually cheaper and sometimes just as nutritious as advertised brands. (Who do you suppose makes the private brands? In many cases the company that makes the advertised brands!) Tuna packed in water will have less fats than those packed in oil which makes water packed tuna the better buy. Why it costs more to package tuna in water is one of the great consumer paradoxes.

Peanut butter

It supplies protein, carbohydrates and vegetable fat—all neces-sary for good growth and energy. Shelf-stable peanut butter (all those nationally advertised brands and maybe even a store brand) is so-called because of all the extras that go into the jar. The first added ingredient you will note is sugar (sometimes listed as dextrose) to make the product palatable (and possibly to mask inferior peanuts), as though it weren't good tasting enough by itself. But mainly you will find hydro-genated oil. This is a solid type shortening, which gives peanut butter its uniform spreading quality. Unlike natural oils, it will not separate and rise to the top of the jar. You can find top quality peanut butter consisting of just peanuts and a dash of salt in your grocery's refrigerated section. It is well worth the extra money. Natural brands which have oil that has risen to the top of the jar are now appearing on the shelf. These simply need a quick stir before using (or simply pour off some or all of the oil). If you refrigerate this natural peanut butter, that will prevent the oil from separating from the spread.

Homemade, Do-it-yourself, Peanut Butter

Make your own. Shell your own peanuts and put a cupful in a blender with a tablespoon of oil—and there you have it! Or you can cheat as I do and buy bags of shelled peanuts—unsalted—to blend into a spread. I should add that peanuts that come shelled often are treated to preserve their freshness. The shell does the same thing naturally.

HINT: 8 Tbsp. of peanut butter equal a ½ cup of peanut butter. Oil spoon or measuring cup before measuring.

The Meaning Of "Lite" on Labels

Light products may or may not have fewer calories, less fat or less sodium. It might be less of one of these three but not necessarily less of all three. Light means different things from product to product. Read the labels and make side by side comparisons.

Breakfast Cereals

Many cereals that children eat are heavily sugared and heavily forti-fied, making them basically a sugar-coated vitamin candy in a cereal bowl rather than a natural food of good fiber. Breakfasting on them is really not a good way to start the day. Avoid those with sugar listed on the package as first ingredient and if possible, second or third. Of course children want to eat them; they taste good, being mainly sugar! If your kids want only King Vitamin, Sugar Smacks or Cocoa Pebbles, and you think that Shredded Wheat and wheat germ are preferable, maybe a middle-of- the-road choice such as Life, Wheaties, Corn Flakes, Cheerios or Rice Krispies would be the best compromise. Keep in mind you can enrich any breakfast cereal by adding toasted wheat germ to it.

There is a way to calculate for yourself, from information right on the cereal box, the percentage of added sugars by weight.

Look down the side panel of practically any box of ready-to-eat cold cereal and you'll find more information than you're probably able to digest. Usually at the bottom of the side panel is a section headed "Carbohydrate Information." Specifically listed here, by grams, is the amount of "Sucrose and Other Sugars" in an ounce of the particular cereal. If you divide this number of grams by 30 (the approximate number of grams in an ounce), you have the percentage of added sugars by weight. Do your calculations just on the cereal information; not on the information under cereal with the milk added.

CARBOHYDRATE INFORMATION		
	Rice Krispies	
	1 Oz. (28.4 g)	With ½ Cup Skim Milk
Starch and Related Carbohydrates	22 g	22 g
Sucrose and Other Sugars	3 g	9 g
Total Carbohydrates	**25 g**	**31 g**

So, if your label lists 3 grams of sucrose and other sugars, it contains 10 percent added sugar.

5 grams is 17 percent sugar
9 grams is 30 percent sugar
12 grams is 40 percent sugar

Select the gram number acceptable to you, and then let your children pick out their own cereal, based on the number they read on the label. You'll be saved a lot of "No, that one is too sugary" answers!

There are many nutritious hot cereals, though I have never been able to get my kids to eat them except for, on occasion, the presweetened, processed instant oatmeal packets. Mine prefer cold whole grain cereals such as granola. While granola is high in calories, owing to the honey and oil used, it is high in natural fiber and nutritional ingredients. Still, check the label, each granola recipe is different. One or two are packaged *without* added salt. Do not delude yourself into

Sucrose and Glucose Content of Commercially Available Cereals

Commercial Cereal Product	Sucrose Content (%)	Glucose Content (%)	Commercial Cereal Product	Sucrose Content (%)	Glucose Content (%)
Shredded Wheat (large biscuit)	1.0	0.2	Granola	16.6	0.6
Shredded Wheat (spoon size biscuit)	1.3	0.3	100% Bran	18.4	0.8
Cheerios	2.2	0.5	All Bran	20.0	1.6
Puffed Rice	2.4	0.4	Granola (with almonds and filberts)	21.4	1.2
Uncle Sam Cereal	2.4	1.2	Fortified Oat Flakes	22.2	1.2
Wheat Chex	2.6	0.9	Heartland	23.1	3.2
Grape Nut Flakes	3.3	0.6	Super Sugar Chex	24.5	0.8
Puffed Wheat	3.5	0.7	Sugar Frosted Flakes	29.0	1.8
Alpen	3.8	4.7	Bran Buds	30.2	2.1
Post Toasties	4.1	1.7	Sugar Sparkled Corn Flakes	32.2	1.8
Product 19	4.1	1.7	Frosted Mini Wheats	33.6	0.4
Corn Total	4.4	1.4	Sugar Pops	37.8	2.9
Special K	4.4	6.4	Alpha bits	40.3	0.6
Wheaties	4.7	4.2	Sir Grapefellow	40.7	3.1
Corn Flakes (Kroger)	5.1	1.5	Super Sugar Crisp	40.7	4.5
Peanut Butter	5.2	1.1	Cocoa Puffs	43.0	3.5
Grape Nuts	6.6	1.1	Cap'n Crunch	43.3	0.8
Corn Flakes (Food Club)	7.0	2.1	Crunch Berries	43.4	1.0
Crispy Rice	7.3	1.5	Kaboom	43.8	3.0
Corn Chex	7.5	0.9	Frankenberry	44.0	2.6
Corn Flakes (Kellogg)	7.8	6.4	Frosted Flakes	44.0	2.9
Total	8.1	1.3	Count Chocula	44.2	3.7
Rice Chex	8.5	1.8	Orange Quangaroos	44.7	0.6
Crisp Rice	8.8	2.1	Quisp	44.9	0.6
Raisin Bran (Skinner)	9.6	9.3	Boo Berry	45.7	2.8
Concentrate	9.9	2.4	Vanilly Crunch	45.8	0.7
Rice Krispies (Kellogg)	10.0	2.9	Baron Von Redberry	45.0	1.5
Raisin Bran (Kellogg)	10.6	14.1	Cocoa Krispies	45.9	0.8
Heartland (with raisins)	13.5	5.6	Trix	46.6	4.1
Buck Wheat	13.6	1.5	Fruit Loops	47.4	0.5
Life	14.5	2.5	Honeycomb	48.8	2.8
Granola (with dates)	14.5	3.2	Pink Panther	49.2	1.3
Granola (with raisins)	14.5	3.8	Cinnamon Crunch	50.3	3.2
Sugar Frosted Corn Flakes	15.6	1.8	Lucky Charms	50.4	7.6
40% Bran Flakes (Post)	15.8	3.0	Cocoa Pebbles	53.5	0.6
Team	15.9	1.1	Apple Jacks	55.0	0.5
Brown Sugar- Cinnamon Frosted Mini Wheats	16.0	0.3	Fruity Pebbles	55.1	1.1
			King Vitamin	58.5	3.1
40% Bran Flakes (Kellogg)	16.2	2.1	Sugar Smacks	61.3	2.4
			Super Orange Crisp	68.0	2.8
			Mean	25.1	2.3
			S.D.	19.16	2.21

Source: *Journal of Dentistry for Children*   Sept.-Oct. 1974

believing that a granola bar with a caramel center is a good breakfast food.

The recipe to make-your-own is on page 91. It's surprisingly easy.

HINT: Serve cereal in a mug with a handle for a change of pace. A new container gives an old regular fresh appeal.

White Flour

When buying flour, you will probably choose between regular white flour and whole wheat flour (see page 21 for additional information). If you purchase white flour, unbleached is preferable. Unbleached simply means that it has gone through one less processing stage which is done for appearance (whitening) only. Once you find the word "unbleached" on a label, look for "enriched." This means that niacin, thiamin, riboflavin and iron have been put back. But these are a replacement of only a few of the many nutrients that have been milled out. So if you are using only white flour and have not yet expanded your horizons, do make sure that you at least purchase the kind which has been enriched. When flour or any product is enriched beyond its original level of nutrients, it is—must be—labeled "fortified." Note that today many flours are being fortified with added calcium.

In reading labels you will notice that everything from pretzels to tomato soup seems to contain flour. Sometimes the flour is enriched, sometimes not. Given a choice between similar products, do buy the one with enriched flour. Sometimes white flour is referred to on labels as wheat flour, which it is. This doesn't mean enriched or whole wheat, just white flour! Don't be deceived.

There is a terrific way to enrich the white flour you use that won't change it's texture or taste. It is called the **CORNELL TRIPLE RICH FORMULA.** Though not a new idea, it is not a commonly used idea—which it should be.

Before putting any flour into your measuring cup, place in the bottom of your one cup measure:

1 Tbsp. soy flour
1 Tbsp. powdered dry milk
1 tsp. regular wheat germ (not the toasted variety)

Then add flour to complete one cup. Mix well. Do this for each cup of flour used. Even whole grain benefits from this formula.

Hint: To make this even easier for yourself, combine the above three ingredients in the same proportions in a large jar and store it in your refrigerator. Then when you need anything enriched, simply take two or three spoonfuls from the jar for each cup of flour and spare yourself opening three containers each time.

You'll notice we said to refrigerate this mixture. Soy flour and wheat germ need refrigeration to prevent them from turning rancid. While dry milk does not become rancid, it can go stale. For this reason, I prefer to buy dry milk that comes in envelopes within a box. If you use lots of dry milk and can go through a box in a month, there is no need to bother with the more expensive packaged "envelope-in-the-box" variety.

Remember that this TRIPLE RICH FORMULA can be used in everything you bake that uses flour: cookies, cakes, breads, waffles, muffins, pancakes, pie-crusts, even some commerical mixes, if used in moderation. Try to make it a habit. It's a good habit that will enrich your family's general nutrition.

Whole Wheat Flour

If you wish to buy completely and naturally enriched flour, buy whole wheat. You may want to purchase whole wheat flour that has been *stone ground*. This means that the whole wheat kernel has been crushed into a fine flour in one process. Absence of the phrase "stone ground whole wheat flour" from the label indicates that the kernel has been milled as for white flour. The bran, wheat germ and center flour kernel were separated and then remixed in proper proportion to give you whole wheat flour. This makes a lighter whole wheat flour but the heat from the extra milling processes destroys many extra nutrients. While preferable to white, do realize that there are variations even in whole wheat flours.

Whole wheat flour actually has a very limited shelf life. Millers expect it to go stale in two to three months, rancid in a year. The oil in the wheat germ is the spoiler. Millers and grocers make a great effort to ensure that the whole wheat flour you buy in the grocery store is as fresh as possible. Once you get it home, store it in your refrigerator or freezer unless you expect to use it promptly.

Interestingly enough, the whole wheat flour and white flour available to us in the grocery are made from two different types of wheat. Whole wheat flour comes from a variety that is 14 percent to 15 percent protein, while our commercial white flour comes from a brand that is 11 percent protein. When the outer bran and wheat germ are milled out of this second type, the resulting white flour has approximately 10 percent protein. Bran and wheat germ are removed so that this lower protein white flour will be a better textured product for baking breads and pastries and have a longer shelf life.

There is also a whole wheat pastry flour (usually found in the health food section) that is made from a softer whole wheat and is similar in texture to white flour. It works well in crusts, bars, cookies, and other such items. It will not rise in yeast breads. If you object to the coarseness of regular whole wheat flour, you may want to experiment with whole wheat pastry flour.

Wheat Germ

Wheat germ, found in the cereal section of your grocery store, is a super food by itself or as an enriching additive. Wheat germ provides a variety of vitamin B's that you could be missing from your diet, especially if you don't eat whole grain breads, yogurt, liver or nutritional brewer's yeast. Wheat germ is so easy to add to foods without detection. Use it to sneak extra good nutrition and fiber into foods your family normally eats. Wheat germ, you will notice, comes two ways—regular and toasted. I buy both. The regular variety is good for use in the CORNELL TRIPLE RICH FORMULA, granola, meat loaf (like bread crumbs), and for enriching innumerable other recipes. Toasted wheat germ, which also works well in granola, is good for toppings. I mix it with chopped peanuts, and sprinkle it in sandwiches and even in salads. Use it wherever you like a sweet and nutty topping. The toasted kind is toasted with honey or sugar, making it more palatable. Remember, after opening, it must be refrigerated.

Buying Bread

If you and your family are hooked on plain white bread, switching will not be easy. First, of course, you must believe that the switch is worthwhile. It takes some effort to read labels and can cost more (good ingredients are more expensive). Look for breads which include whole grains among the primary ingredients. Check the label for caramel coloring because some breads are made with it to look like whole grain breads when they are not. Also, make the switch gradually. Experiment until you find a bread you can live with. Some families move to coarser breads gradually. Others find themselves making sandwiches using whole wheat for one piece of the sandwich and white bread for the other as part of their transition to more wholesome breads. Because whole grain breads are more filling, you may not need to buy as much bread and the cost can equal out. You will notice this when you make sure you are buying bread by weight and not size. Breads made with milk, whole or powdered, supply added nutrients.

Another nutritional choice in bread is *Pita* bread, also known as *pocket bread* or *Syrian flat bread*. This is bread dough shaped in a flat circle. When baked it provides a hidden pocket between the thin crusts. It is available as whole wheat or white bread. It is a low calorie bread containing no fats, no shortening and no preservatives. Most anything can be stuffed in the pockets when the bread is cut in half: sloppy joes, taco filling, hamburger, pizza makings, deli-meats, chili, sausage and onions, scrambled eggs and bacon—you name it! When split open they even make a good crust for an individual pizza.

Buy some or make your own!

Pita Bread

1 pkg. yeast
1-¼ cup lukewarm water
2 tsp. salt

3 cups flour (white, whole wheat or any combination)

Dissolve yeast in the lukewarm water. Stir in flour and salt. Stir into a rough sticky ball. Knead on floured board until smooth, adding flour if necessary. Divide into six balls and knead each ball until smooth and round. With a rolling pin, flatten each until ¼-inch thick and about four or five inches in diameter. Cover with a towel and let rise 45 minutes. Arrange the rounds upside down on baking sheets. Bake in a very hot oven (500°) for 10-15 minutes or until browned and puffed in the center.

The breads will be hard when they are removed from the oven, but will soften and flatten as they cool. For sandwiches, split carefully and fill with any combination of sandwich makings.

Oatmeal

Oatmeal processed as rolled oats is a popular grain that is probably better liked in cookies than in the cereal bowl. It contains much good food value in whatever form it is eaten. Oatmeal contains the bran and germ of the oat, and little nutritional value is lost when it is milled in the rolling process. It also provides good fiber. The steel cut variety is the most nutritious but it requires an hour to cook. Its slightly less nutritious cousin, known as "old fashioned" oats, cooks up in five minutes. Avoid the one minute kind as extra food value is eliminated during its manufacture. Oatmeal is terrific in cookies, bars, breads, granolas, toppings and, yes, even as a bowl of hot cereal. It is felt by some that the water-soluble fiber found in oats may be responsible for a cholesterol-lowering effect in modified-fat diets.

- Make oat flour by running it in your blender or food processor for a minute at the "grind" setting.
- Use as a ⅓ replacement for bread crumbs in meatloaf.
- Add a few spoonfuls when making a sloppy joe mixture.
- Toast with a bit of margarine and cinnamon to make a crunchy topping for fruit or ice cream.

Cookies

Walking down the cookie aisle, which always seems to be next to the candy section, is usually an ordeal with children along. My basic approach to buying commercial cookies is to choose those with redeeming value having fillings such as peanut butter, figs, or other fruit fillings or to buy cookies made with whole grain flours or oatmeal as their major ingredients. Did you know that graham crackers with different but similar names on their boxes have different proportionate ingredients? Following is a list of three kinds of Nabisco Graham Crackers and the order of ingredients listed on their boxes:

Cinnamon Grahams: Enriched wheat flour, sugar, shortening, graham flour, high fructose corn syrup, molasses, honey, corn syrup, baking soda, dextrose, salt, and cinnamon.

Honey Maid: Enriched wheat flour, sugar, shortening, graham flour, honey, high fructose corn syrup, salt, leavening and artificial flavor.

Graham Crackers: Enriched wheat flour, graham flour, rye flour, sugar, shortening, molasses, corn sweeteners, salt and leavening.

I don't know about you, but I would certainly vote for the last one. Also, here is an instance where the wheat flour mentioned refers to white flour and not whole wheat flour.

Cream-filled cookies are usually high in sugar. Pepperidge Farm cookies, while expensive, are made with good quality ingredients. Their Short Bread Cookies and Date Nut Granola Cookies are relatively low in sugar content. All Pepperidge Farm Cookies contain no artificial colorings, flavorings or preservatives. This is not true of most cookie manufacturers.

Crackers

Generally crackers can be a good substitute for cookies if you stay away from the heavily salted kind. The variety in stores is large. Check them out! Melba-toast, Stoned Wheat Thins, even snack crackers tend to provide a good variety of grain flours and much less sugar. Many are now being offered with less salt.

Ritz Crackers have less sugar than cookies but are not sugar-free. Saltines are sugar-free but not salt-free. Of the saltines, Premium brand contains the least salt, as indicated by a comparison of box labels.

Commercial Baby Food

Commercial baby foods are often high in water content and low in solid content. The foods appear solid because tapioca and modified starches are added as thickeners. Digestibility of modified starches by babies is debatable. The starches are not harmful but they may limit absorption of the major food content. A jar may contain 60 percent fruit and 40 percent water thickened to look uniform throughout. Avoid paying fruit and vegetable prices for modified starches and water. The added sugar in junior baby foods and desserts—aimed at the parents' taste buds, primarily—results in the early development of a sweet tooth, contributing to future obesity and tooth decay. Avoid baby juices with added sugar. Juice is sweet to begin with. Remember that regular unsweetened apple juice is already "strained."

Most of us use commercial baby foods at times. How does one pick and choose from the vast array of products? First, remember that most doctors today agree that until they are four to six months of age, babies do not need solid foods. Mother's milk or formula provides everything most full-term babies need until then. Cereal is a good first food because it is a good source of iron. Iron is low in mother's milk and in the regular formula you buy ready-to-feed. The American Academy of Pediatrics now recommends iron-fortified formula for babies from two to 12 months old. When the time comes to use pureed foods and you are not making your own, choose from single basic fruits, vegetables and meats. Avoid sugar, salt and modified starches in commercial baby food by reading labels and being selective in your purchases.

Avoid baby food desserts, combination dinners and foods that you can buy better and cheaper in their natural state elsewhere in the grocery store. For example, mash your own banana (and talk about a good container, it's even unbreakable if dropped) instead of buying strained bananas.

It is important to get your babies off to a good start while you have total control of their dietary intake.

Dairy

There is skim milk, regular milk and milks with varying butterfat content. All are fortified with vitamins A and D. So milk is a good source of some vitamins and calcium and—remember this—*a lot of protein*!

One percent milk has 1 percent butterfat; two percent milk has 2 percent butterfat; and whole milk has 3-¼ percent butterfat. Skim milk is exactly the same as other milk but without any butterfat. Since our diets tend to be fat-laden enough, skim milk is probably the best for all of us. You will find that opinions vary here. The main exception is under the age of two years. If you think you need to cut back on your child's calories (and your doctor agreed with you), do it elsewhere, not here. That extra butterfat is important to early growth and development.

Powdered non-fat milk is an economical way to purchase milk. You reconstitute it yourself. The most frequent complaint is that it tastes like it has been reconstituted. To avoid this, mix the reconstituted powdered milk in a blender and let it stand in the refrigerator at least 12 hours before using. At the very least, you can use reconstituted milk when cooking and baking.

Yogurt

Yogurt has gone from a food once thought of only as a health food fad to a popular food competing for shelf space in every grocery store in the country.

Yogurt is milk cultured by live bacteria. In fact, without bacteria it isn't really yogurt. There is no federal standard for yogurt so bacteria counts vary. All ingredients are listed on the container. The common base ingredient is cultured lowfat milk, and milk or skim milk solids. Different companies add different "thickeners" to their products. Some companies add gelatin. Others add modified food starch, citric acid, or sodium caseinate. Despite the fact that it is made with lowfat milk solids, there are 150 calories in a container of plain yogurt; over 200 calories in the fruited kind.

There are all those yummy flavors. Unfortunately, most are made up of artificial colorings and flavorings and added sugar. Some companies even pasteurize yogurt which kills off all the bacteria—and bacteria is what yogurt is all about.

If you are not bothering to check labels, most fancy flavored commercial yogurts should be viewed as a better-for-you, high-caloried dairy treat rather than for its value as a cultured yogurt. But that still leaves it providing a lot of protein and calcium. The frozen yogurts also lose their bacteria value through freezing but they still have ½ the calories of regular ice cream.

Plain yogurt combines well with many foods, if you don't enjoy it plain. It can be used:

- as a popsicle base
- combined with fresh fruits
- mixed with tuna or clams for a dip
- combined with ricotta cheese when making Lasagne
- substituted for milk in souffles or omlettes
- instead of sour cream
- as a topping for pies or pancakes
- as a salad dressing

Eggs

Eggs are a terrific food. All sorts of good nutrients lie packaged in that well-designed shell. On a cost per serving basis it is most inexpensive. If there is less than a 7 cent price spread between one size and the next, buy the larger size.

To tell if an egg in the shell is raw or hard-cooked, spin it on a flat surface. If it spins fast and easily, it is hard-cooked. If it wobbles, it's raw.

Eggs high cholesterol count makes it a controversial food. Don't serve eggs every day. Maybe you wish to think of it in terms of one carton of eggs a week for your family of four, as one type of guideline. The cholesterol problem lies in the yolk not the white, so make an omelette with two whites and one yolk and let your dog enjoy the extra yolk on those occasions.

If you have run out of ideas on new ways to entice your children to eat eggs when you are serving them, may I suggest:

Green Eggs And Ham

Beat one or two eggs well and add a drop or two of *blue* food coloring before cooking in a pan. Add a slice (or cubes) of leftover ham. Dr. Suess will love you for it!

Cheese

Cheeses are a readily available source of calcium and protein, usually well received, by rapidly growing children. Hard and natural cheeses are a better food value than processed cheese. Processed cheeses cost less, have more additives and are processed with water; ergo, you pay for higher water content. Natural cheeses are made from milk solids. Natural cheeses in hunks will give you your best dollar buy. The sharper the flavor of cheese the higher the price. Domestic cheeses tend to be less expensive than imported ones.

Cheese is a very nutritious food. Unfortunately it can also be high in fat, cholesterol and sodium. This is especially true of processed cheeses. Look for cheeses made from skimmed milk, or those which have "low-fat cheese" written on the label. This goes for cottage cheese too. If you have bought regular creamed cottage cheese, you can rinse it off with water in a strainer to reduce its fat content.

You can make processed cheeses "go farther" if you serve them grated, rather than in chunks, on pizzas, salads, sandwiches and the like.

Cream cheese, I'm sorry to say, is not a good source of protein. Do not equate it with other cheeses. It offers more in fat than protein. Think of it in the same terms as butter or margarine. Serve it with higher protein foods such as peanut butter, or sliced turkey rather than just with jelly. Whipped cream cheese has air whipped in to increase its volume which means you'll spread the fat content and have less fat per bite.

Hint: Enrich the food value of cream cheese by adding one table-spoon of powdered milk to one 8 ounce package.

Beverages

Any canned beverage which says "Drink" or "-ade" on the label is telling you that you are buying mainly water. No doubt the next ingredient is sugar followed by artificial flavorings and colorings. The manufacturer might even throw in some real juice. If you buy a 46 oz. can with 10 percent juice for 95 cents, that means that you have to buy 10 cans to get one whole quart of 100 percent fruit juice. Just think, you are paying $9.50 a quart to get the equivalent fruit juice can. A similar size can of apple juice is about $1.30 and one of pineapple juice is $1.40.

Now if you aren't thinking in terms of buying fruit juice, why not just add sugar to your own water and throw in some artificial colorings and flavorings?

When you buy the real thing—fruit juice, that is—you are getting a bargain because all the vitamins, minerals and natural fruit carbohydrates (versus refined sugar) are present at no extra cost. A label will state "pure fruit juice." If it says "juice" only, then it may be but 50 percent juice. If it says "drink" then it will be no more than 10 percent juice. Apple juice (and make sure that the label does not say "added sugar") and grape juice are two favorite no-sugar-added juices available in bottles. The frozen grape juice concentrate in cans does have some sugar added while grape juice in bottles does not. If a juice label says it's 10 percent juice—remember that means it is 90 percent added water.

If you need to stretch your own fruit juice, do so by adding five parts water to one part fresh fruit juice. Add sweetener to taste.

When purchasing soda pop, do remember that again you are buying water, bubbles, sugar, colorings and flavorings. Granted they taste good and seem to satisfy thirst, but they provide a tremendous amount of calories with no nutritional benefit. For the most part, clear sugar free drinks such as the lemon and lime type and 7-UP™ (regular and sugar-free) tend to use no artificial colorings and flavorings. Read the labels. It's all written out for you...albeit in very small print. A glass of ginger ale contains six to eight teaspoons of sugar. You would not put that much sugar in your own coffee or tea and yet these beverages are served to our children without a second thought.

Natural sodas are basically natural flavors or fruit juices with carbonated water. Most natural sodas have sweetener added. They are not usually low in calories.

Mineral Waters

Bottled water seems to be the new health drink. It is certainly a good trend away from the sugars and artificial colorings and caffeine choices we have been limited to. It is expensive, as you will discover if you or one of your children start to drink several bottles a day.

Packaged Drinks

Here is one area where modern packaging has changed our choices overnight. Boxed and foil-packed drinks are a wonderful convenience drink for lunches, traveling, outings and the like. But like every other drink in that section of the grocery, you can make intelligent choices. The cheaper choices are going to offer you less from a nutritional standpoint. Juice simply costs more than packaged, flavored water.

Hot Dogs

Just a few words about hot dogs. They have come under attack owing to the inclusion of sodium nitrites, a questionable additive also used in many luncheon meats, ham and other cured meat products. This additive prevents botulism (food poisoning) and gives a reddish color to the products it's used in.

Nitrites in large doses can be toxic but they are used in very, very small quantities in hot dogs as a preservative and coloring agent. Nitrites and nitrates occur naturally in many foods we eat. Most green vegetables (lettuce, spinach) contain nitrates in higher amounts than is allowed as additives to foods. The concern is not about the nitrites themselves but because they can form nitrosamines which in large amounts have proved to be cancer-causing.

Confusing? Even the experts trying to determine the safety of this additive are divided on the issue. I think it is reasonable to limit our consumption of foods containing sodium nitrite. Hot dogs once a week, I think, are not a problem. However, bacon for breakfast, hot dogs for lunch, ham for dinner and beef jerky for snacks might well constitute one. A better reason to avoid serving hot dogs is their high fat content. The average hot dog is 29 percent fat by weight, and high fat content in the American diet contributes to heart disease—the number one cause of death in the United States.

Freezer Section

The freezer section of the supermarket is part of today's miracle. Still, as everywhere else in the store, selective shopping is the key. Some best buys for food value in the frozen food section are:

Frozen juice concentrates
Frozen vegetables in large bags
Fish (and I do not mean fish sticks)
Turkey
Lasagna dinners
Plain cheese pizzas
Frozen fruits (packed without sugar)
Frozen whole wheat bread or bread dough
Frozen corn and whole wheat muffins
Quality ice creams made with natural ingredients
Frozen juice bars

Frozen dinners have taken significant strides in the last few years offering us tasty, balanced meals in new varieties.

Well, enough of our trip through the grocery store. I certainly did not cover everything but I have tried to touch on foods that those of us with small children gravitate towards. For a much more complete guide. I recommend *"The Supermarket Handbook"* by Nikki and David Goldbeck (Signet, 1976), $3.95.

As I look back over my comments I see that I often mention products that could cost you more. I don't think that buying better will cost you less but I don't believe it has to cost you more, either. When you buy apple juice instead of soda pop, peanut butter with natural ingredients versus luncheon meats, a hunk of cheese instead of two packages of chips, you will probably come out the same. Your variety may not be quite as wide as in the past but the quality will certainly be better.

And speaking of money, a few last words about living within a budget at the grocery store. I don't know whether it is really possible. Articles I've read about folks who pass on such information in women's magazines (usually the family of eight is living on $50 worth of monthly groceries) has never translated well for me. In fact, I find that a neighborhood grocery which provides the most economical buys for one of my neighbors doesn't do so for me. It all depends on what you intend to buy, and only you can do a cost comparison on that.

As for grocery store coupons, they may save you money, but beware! Do you realize that only a small portion of them ever offer values on basic foods? They are usually offered on convenience and packaged foods and non-food products (thanks to the manufacturers) rather than on your meats, produce and dairy items.

While waiting in the check-out line you can always play my favorite supermarket game "What's Your Bag?" Just casually eye the contents of the grocery cart next to yours. Try not to be obvious; you don't want to appear nosey. There's a lot you can learn about the life-style of other shoppers. Do they have a large family or are they single? Do they own a dog or a cat? Do they entertain lavishly or frugally? But, more important, can you size up their nutrition consciousness? Do you see whole grain or white flour products? Fresh produce or canned goods? Cans of soda pop, fruit drinks or juice? Candy bars or dried fruit snacks? This is a very revealing "game." Remember that the next time you notice someone eyeing your grocery cart.

YOU CAN'T EAT THIS BECAUSE I LOVE YOU AND I WANT YOU TO GROW UP STRONG AND HEALTHY.

WEIGHTS AND MEASURES

MILK SUBSTITUTES

Baking and run out of milk or cream? Remember that:

If the recipe calls for: **You can substitute:**

1 cup coffee cream   3 tablespoons butter plus ⅞ cup milk

1 cup heavy cream   ⅓ cup butter plus ¾ cup milk

1 cup whole milk   1 cup reconstituted non-fat dry milk
                                                 plus 2½ teaspoons butter or margarine
                                                 or
                                                 ½ cup evaporated milk plus ½ cup water

1 cup buttermilk or juice   1 tablespoon vinegar or lemon juice
                                                 plus enough sweet milk to make 1 cup
                                                 (let stand 5 minutes before using)

FOOD EQUIVALENTS FOR MILK

1 cup buttermilk	=	1 cup milk
1 cup yogurt	=	1 cup milk
½ cup ice cream	=	1/4 cup milk
½ cup ice milk	=	⅓ cup milk
1 cup baked custard	=	1 cup milk
1 ounce (slice) Swiss cheese	=	1 cup milk
1 slice American processed cheese	=	½ cup milk
1 inch cube cheddar cheese	=	½ cup milk
1 cup cottage cheese (creamed)	=	⅓ cup milk
2 tablespoons cream cheese	=	1 tablespoon milk

TO USE HONEY INSTEAD OF SUGAR WHEN BAKING

- Use ⅔ cup of honey for each cup of sugar called for.
- For each cup of honey that you use, deduct about 3 tablespoons of liquid for the recipe. (This does not apply to yeast bread.) In baked goods — add ½ teaspoon soda for every cup substituted.
- Reduce oven temperature by about 25 degrees and bake a little longer as honey tends to make baked goods brown faster.

  To use honey instead of brown sugar, use some molasses with the honey.

MEASURE FOR MEASURE

1 pound flour	=	4 cups
1 stick or ¼ pound butter	=	½ cup
1 square chocolate	=	1 ounce
14 squares graham crackers	=	1 cup fine crumbs
1½ slices bread	=	1 cup soft crumbs
4 ounces macaroni (1-1¼ cups)	=	2¼ cups cooked
4 ounces noodles (1½-2 cups)	=	2 cups cooked
1 cup long grain rice	=	3-4 cups cooked
juice of one lemon	=	3 tablespoons
grated peel of 1 lemon	=	1 teaspoon
juice of one orange	=	⅓ cup
grated peel of 1 orange	=	2 teaspoons
1 medium apple, chopped	=	1 cup
1 medium banana, mashed	=	⅓ cup
1 pound American cheese (shredded)	=	4 cups
1 pound raisins	=	3½ cups
1 pound carrots	=	4 medium or 6 small 3 cups shredded 2½ cups diced
1 cup milk	=	½ cup evaporated milk plus ½ cup water OR ⅓ cup dry milk plus one cup water
1 cup sour milk	=	1 teaspoon vinegar or lemon juice plus fresh milk to make 1 cup (let stand 5 minutes before using)

WEIGHTS AND MEASURES

3 teaspoons	=	1 tablespoon
4 tablespoons	=	¼ cup
8 tablespoons	=	½ cup
16 tablespoons	=	1 cup
1 cup	=	8 ounces
1 cup	=	½ pint
2 cups	=	1 pint
2 pints	=	1 quart
4 cups	=	1 quart
4 quarts	=	1 gallon

SIZE OF CAN

8 ounces	=	1 cup
9 ounces	=	No. 1 flat or 1 cup
16 ounces	=	No. 1 tall or 2 cups
16 ounces	=	No. 303
12 ounces	=	No. 2 vacuum or 1¾ cups
20 ounces (18 fluid)	=	No. 2 or 2½ cups
28 ounces	=	No. 2½ or 3½ cups
46 ounces	=	No. 3 cylinder or 5¾ cups
6 lbs. 10 ounces	=	No. 10 or 13 cups

INDEX